ASTRO-METEOROLOGY

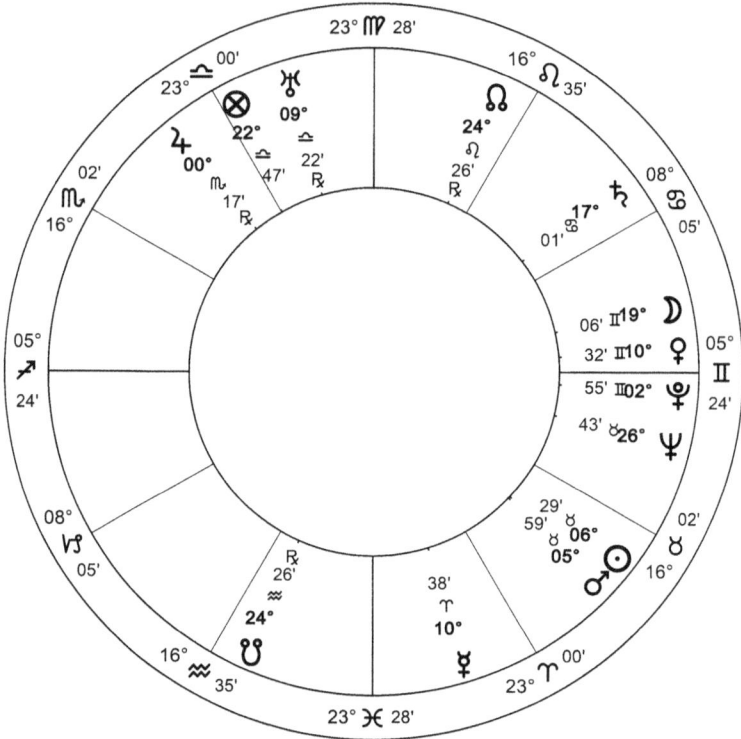

Natal chart of George J. McCormack
April 26, 1887
9:17 pm LMT
Springfield, Massachusetts
Source: Holden and Hughes, <u>Astrological Pioneers of America</u>, AFA, 1988

A Textbook

of

Long Range Weather Forecasting

by
George J. McCormack

Astrology Classics

To Elizabeth, on her birthday, with love.

My thanks to Philip Graves, of Sweden, for use of his copy.
Thanks also to Carolyn Egan, the Weather Sage for her extract of A.J. Pearce's
Text-Book, and for McCormack's A Brief History of Astrometeorology

On the cover: Kansas tornado, Stormy skies, both from a Chinese wallpaper site.

This book was first published in 1947, by the author himself, in an edition limited to 100 copies. The copy from which this edition was made was composed of 59 hand-typed, single-spaced, one-sided letter-sized pages, bound in a blue 3-ring binder. The 100 copies — a life's work — were very nearly lost altogether.

ISBN: 978 1 933303 45 1

Published by
Astrology Classics

The publication division of
The Astrology Center of America
207 Victory Lane, Bel Air MD 21014

On the net at www.**AstroAmerica.com**

Table of Contents

Foreword:
Astrology Under Our Feet
by David R. Roell

I was working on a theory of astrology when, in January 2011, Parke Kunkle, of the Minnesota Planetarium Society, casually repeated an old story, that there were really 13 signs of the zodiac, not twelve. Thus inspired, I redoubled my efforts. As long as it has existed, Astrology has been a puzzle with multiple unknowns, hence the real difficulty in making sense of it. I was further inspired by George McCormack's extraordinary book, the one you now hold in your hands. His observations fit my theory so closely that I dare to venture an overview of my work here, in the hopes that my theory and McCormack's observations may combine in some useful way.

The Tropical Zodiac

McCormack uses the Tropical Zodiac in his work. The tropical zodiac is based on the Earth-Sun relationship, specifically, declinations and seasons. Aries starts the spring season, Cancer the summer, Libra autumn, and Capricorn, winter. These are calculated as of the moment the Sun appears to cross the Earth's equator, or achieves maximum north or south declination.

The length of each season is based on the dates of the Earth's apogee and perigee, the Earth's closest and furthest approaches to the Sun. As these dates slowly drift over time, the exact length of each season, in days, hours, minutes, and seconds, slowly change over the centuries. While the length of the year remains exactly the same, its seasonal divisions do not. The four seasons are not of exactly equal length. Most likely, they never have been. In 2012, the Earth was at perihelion on January 5, and at aphelion on July 5. In 1837, these dates were January 2 and July 1. (*Source*: Tables of Planetary Phenomena, 3rd edition, 2007, by Michelsen and Pottenger)

The start of the four seasons are represented by the four elements: Fire, for spring; water, for summer; air, for autumn; and earth for winter. Each of the seasons were then trisected to show the three states of energy they embodied: Active, or Cardinal; followed by Immoveable, or Fixed; and then, No energy, which we know as Mutable. Whereupon the next season arrived to restart the energy matrix. An element was then assigned to each third of a season, resulting in a year of four seasons and twelve segments (months), which became the signs of the Zodiac.

This is a precise method, and an unvarying one. The Zodiac is thus a 4 x 3 grid, of energies mapped against elements. There are only twelve signs. There could only ever be twelve. Not thirteen.

There is an old story that Libra and Scorpio were once joined as a single sign. This was presumably an attempt to suppress Scorpio as "evil". The inherent structure of the Zodiac makes eleven signs impossible.

This structure means the Tropical Zodiac is not *of* the sky, nor *in* the sky, but **expresses the relationship between Earth and Sun.**

Can we determine if the Zodiac is geocentric or heliocentric?

Yes, we can. First, we note that as we are talking of ourselves, the Zodiac we create will presumably be created of ourselves. Of the Earth, in other words. A plant, for example, grows *from* the Earth, but grows *because* of the Sun's light and heat. So is the plant of the Earth, or is it of the Sun? The answer is that the plant is *of* the Earth, but is *nurtured* by the Sun. The plant is therefore a subset of the Earth. It is the Earth's response to the Sun's energy. In its own unique way, the plant shows the Earth-Sun relationship.

We do the same analysis with the elements and energies that make up the Zodiac. Where can they properly be found? The Earth contains all four elements, fire, earth, air and water. The Sun has only fire. The Earth also has all three states of energy: Cardinal, Fixed and none. The Sun has only Cardinal. By comparison, the sky has neither elements nor energies. Therefore,

The signs of the Zodiac are qualities inherent in the Earth itself.

Astrology is Earth-based.

The Tropical Zodiac has nothing to do with the sky. Never has, and never will. Presumably the Zodiac was projected into the sky at some point as a reference, as in, *See this constellation overhead at midnight? When the Sun gets to it, it will be summer again.* (The Sidereal Zodiac has a different explanation. It is not based on stars, but the Moon.)

If the Zodiac is not of the sky but are qualities inherent in the Earth itself, then it is reasonable to expect the Earth would express these twelve basic qualities. Indeed, the word *zodiac* itself relates to animals, which are of the Earth. Traditionally it is said that Aries is symbolized by the ram, that Taurus is symbolized by the ox, etc., but it is more penetrating to say the Earth **expresses** its Aries energy *as* a ram, its Taurus energy as an ox, its Cancer energy as a crab, its Leo energy as a lion, etc. If qualities are inherent in the clay of the Earth itself, then it is natural the Earth would express them. By contrast, if astrological energies were external to the Earth, then the Earth's response would be *in reaction* to them. Sometimes agreeable and compatible, sometimes hostile and maladroit.

This analysis can be taken further. Medical astrology holds that different parts of the body are ruled by different signs. If the ruling signs are external to the

Earth, then the Earth's reaction to them will produce maladjusted, maladroit results. Only if these qualities are *inherent in the Earth*, can the Earth produce perfect results, since those results will be in keeping with the fundamental qualities of the Earth and will be as perfect as the Earth, no more and no less.

In other words, the eyes, which in all creatures are found in pairs, are ruled by the Sun and Moon, the two light-givers, as represented by Leo and Cancer. Because it is the Earth which produces Leo and Cancer, the eyes the Earth produce see as well as the Earth can make them see. Likewise hands, which are ruled by Virgo, feet, which are ruled by Pisces, ankles, which are ruled by Aquarius, the heart, ruled by Leo, etc. In every creature, no matter where in the overall scheme of things, each and every part is a miracle of perfection. Never mere adaptations or make-dos. Because the Earth is made up of Leo and Aquarius and Cancer and Taurus and all the rest, it expertly combines the various parts to make the creatures which inhabit the planet. Precisely the same can be said for the Earth's plants, gems and minerals. Will everything on Earth perfectly express its inherent Zodiacal sign energies? Of course not, because the Earth itself is not perfect. There is a great deal of, well, dirt, and always will be. A painter leaves paint on his palette, a baker leaves flour behind on his counter, etc. No process is without waste.

Planets

While Astrology may be *of* the Earth, may be *in* the Earth, may be the very *life of the Earth*, by itself the Earth and its astrology are *static* and *unchanging*.

In reality the Earth is but one of a number of planets in orbit around the Sun and therefore must by definition be in continuous and ongoing relationship with each and every planetary body in the solar system. Mars, for example, may not have a direct impact upon me, but, as a planet, Mars is more than big enough, more than close enough, more than fast enough, to have an impact upon the Earth as a whole. Just as I would expect the Earth to influence Mars.

These interplanetary relationships are by means of *harmony* and *resonance*. Mars has its own harmonies and resonances, its own "style" and "personality" as it were. The ceaseless interplay of Earth and Mars will excite, in each planet, those elements and energies which are in sympathy or harmony. In other words, Mars will, in one fashion or another, "illuminate" or identify the energies in the Earth which are in resonance with it. In a larger sense, every part of the Earth will react, in one way or another, to the energies of Mars, taken as a whole. In other words, speaking broadly, Mars likes Aries and Scorpio the best, gets on well with Capricorn, but dislikes Libra, Taurus and Cancer.

As with Mars, so with all the planets. In addition to whole signs, there are various sub-frequencies, among them, day/night rulers, triplicity rulers, decans, faces, terms/bounds, dwads, etc. Indeed, we can say, collectively, that we only know Terrestrial energies, the signs of the Zodiac themselves, by means of their resonance with the various planets. Energies in the Earth which are not in some way "triggered" by the various planets will therefore be latent, unexpressed and unknown.

So we now have an Earth with its own unique Zodiacal energies, which are stimulated, excited, *brought into being*, by the various planets, the resulting vibrations so thoroughly mixed that it is pervasive in every rock, every spade of soil, in the very clay of our own bodies. While it is true that Mars has no *gravitational* effect upon any of us, it is also true that *because* we are made of the Earth, *because* we are made of material which is itself vibrating, we not only resonate to the Earth's own vibrations, but, we, each of us, also vibrate directly and individually to Mars. And, as before, with all the other planets.

Is distance a factor? Yes it is. Broadly speaking, the closer planets will be more nuanced and more detailed, with the Moon being the most nuanced and the most detailed. And in fact, in astrology, the inner planets (Sun, Moon, Mercury, Venus, Mars) are known as *personal*. Jupiter and Saturn, which are much further away, are *social*. The outer planets are *generational*. Outer planets only "step forward" when in close aspect with inner planets.

We have now arrived at a second fundamental principle:

The interplay of Earth and planets produce astrology as we know it.

The signs of the Zodiac are *in the Earth*. They are *brought to life* by the Earth's ceaseless interaction with the other planets. This makes the Earth a giant vibrating sphere, and it is on this sphere that we live.

A number of things have now become quite simple. Why is birth a critical moment? Here is an analogy. Imagine the Earth to be like a vibrating, orbital sander. Orbital sanders are hand-held electrical devices for smoothing wood. They have a flat pad on the bottom where the sandpaper is secured.

Take the sandpaper off and turn the unit upside down, that is, with the flat side up. Put a penny on the sander, and turn it on. The vibrating sander is the Earth. The penny is you. Both the sander and the penny are vibrating, with similar, but as we can see, not quite identical vibrations.

Now consider the Earth's vibration, unlike that of the sander's, is not consistent, but variable, and this because of the Earth's ceaseless relationship with the Sun, Moon and other planets. With the sander in your hand, carefully tilt it this way and that. Note how the penny reacts to every change. Move too abruptly and the penny will fly off the sander. Which, by analogy, is to say that when the Earth's vibration becomes too intense, we have accidents, we sicken and die.

Replace the penny with, say, a cookie and turn the sander on again. Run the sander until the cookie has become so distressed that it starts to break up. Note how each separating fragment takes on the sander's vibration as of the moment of its separation. Note how the main fragment changes its vibration after every loss. *This is a precise analogy to a mother giving birth to a child.* Note the subsequent interactions among the various pieces. Based on their location, mass and the specific vibrations as of the moment of separation, pieces will collide with other pieces at stated times and places. Astrologically this is known as synastry.

The initial vibration of all objects age, or *decay*, over time. In astrology, we "age" an individual's "vibration" (aka natal chart) by means of primary directions, secondary directions and solar arcs, among other means. (In India, by Vimshottari dashas, etc.) The relationship and interaction of decayed vibrations with transits is therefore obvious.

Note in this theory, a tree, precisely because it is firmly connected to the Earth, cannot be said to have a "birthday" as it never separates from the Earth.

Aspects

We might say that, yes, there are aspects between the planets. Why wouldn't there be aspects, when planets come to simple angular relationships among themselves? Regrettably, there are two problems with this.

One, while we have established the Zodiac to be in the Earth itself, this Zodiac is based not on longitude, but rather on the *Sun's declination.* If the Sun is at $21^{\circ}37'$ S declination, then its longitude is $22^{\circ}13'57"$ of Capricorn and the date is more or less January 13 of any given year. (The leap year messes up the date slightly, this example is from 1950 and a midnight ephemeris.)

Moreover it is not entirely clear if this declination to longitude exchange should be based upon the Earth (geocentric) or the Sun (heliocentric).

The second problem is that Ptolemaic aspects, for heretofore mysterious and unknown reasons, are all centered around 60°. To these, George McCormack adds 30° and 45°, which is to say, half of 60, and half the distance between 30 and 60. With 30 we are immediately reminded of the twelve houses, which, ideally, are 30° each, which then reminds us of the signs, which, when projected into the sky, are also 30° each. We are being led, or, perhaps pushed, into some sort of definite structure. And it seems that we have a solution.

Researchers Ronald Cohen and Lars Stixrude, at the Carnegie Institution of Washington, have recently postulated the central core of the Earth to be a single giant crystal. Exactly what kind of crystal they have not yet determined, but they are leaning in favor of the crystal being hexagonal. Which is six-sided.

And in fact there is a variation of iron and nickel that forms hexagonal crystals. It is found in meteorites. Which, as everyone knows, are the remains of destroyed planets, presumably their cores. That substance is **hexahedrite**.

Upon learning of hexahedrite I was at first disappointed, as I wanted the Earth to have a twelve-sided crystal. One that would explain twelve signs and twelve houses, etc. But while looking at pictures of crystals on-line, I glanced at one too many pictures of crystalline water, in other words, snowflakes. And then it hit me.

The hexagonal crystal does not express six, but rather, twelve.

How does a six-sided crystal express twelve? Quite simply. Look at a crystal. You will find both facets and edges. Six-sided crystals have six of each. We might arbitrarily label them as six masculine edges and six feminine facets, or vice-versa. Which, to the Earth, are the six masculine signs (Aries, Gemini, Leo, Libra, Sagittarius, Aquarius) and six feminine (Taurus, Cancer, Virgo, Scorpio, Capricorn, Pisces). The hexagonal crystal at the center of the Earth, precisely because it is hexagonal, describes astrology as we know it. Describes the twelve-fold division of the Zodiac, describes the masculine-feminine polarities, and describes the innate nature of the traditional Ptolemaic aspects. All of which are based 30° and 60°.

This permits us to state a third principle:

Astrology may be defined as qualities inherent in, and the further study of, the six sided crystal at the center of the Earth.

Being the core of the Earth itself, the Earth's central hexagonal crystal is presumably aligned with the Earth's axial tilt of 23°44'. If so, then because this tilt is always in the same direction, we have the reason why 0° of Aries is set to the spring Equinox. The Equinox is the Earth's annual "re-centering" or "realigning" with the Sun. Projecting this hexagonal alignment into the sky lets us map the planets in the solar system from the Earth's own, unique, point of view. It gives us the geocentric, Tropical, Zodiac. We are mapping *the Earth's* relationship to the various other bodies in the solar system. We are not mapping the Sun, so we are not heliocentric.

Nor are we concerned with the Sidereal Zodiac, which is based, not on fixed stars, but on the Earth's axial wobble. This wobble is due to various gravitational influences on the Earth, most notably the fight between the Sun and Moon. Like as not, if there was no Moon, there would be no wobble and therefore no Sidereal Zodiac, or perhaps, one that was so slow in motion as to be impracticable. (The Sidereal Zodiac moves at the rate of 1 degree every 72 years, which is a cycle of 25,920 years, more or less.)

It is, in fact, the *projection* of the Tropical Zodiac, from the Earth, into the sky, that enables us to finally *identify and name* the Zodiacal energies *inside* the Earth itself. We do not know what the Earth's Aries energy may be, except that it is "illuminated" or "triggered" when planets pass through the section of sky which the Earth's Equinoctial settings have labeled as "Aries". This transference explains the traditional confusion about astrology, about what and where it really is and how it really works. It is almost impossible to see "Aries" in the Earth itself, but it is easy to see its *projection* into the sky.

So the *common* influence of the planets on the Earth, which is that Mars, for example, rules Aries and Scorpio, etc., becomes *dynamic* as the planet Mars moves about in space and appears to enter one sign after another. As it enters the various signs, as it shifts from "pushing" on a facet of the Earth's central crystal (at its spring alignment) to "pulling" on an edge between two facets, its vibratory impact upon the Earth changes accordingly. In common parlance, we say that Mars rules Aries from its current position in, for example, the sign of Leo.

Now note that the hexagonal crystal explains not only the twelve *signs*, but in the daily rotation of the Earth's axis, the twelve *houses* as well. Note that while the Zodiac is a matter of simple longitude, astrological houses are customarily calculated according to the Earth's horizon and Prime Vertical. *Not* (with the exception of Porphyry houses, an early and crude system) according to zodiacal longitude. With this minor tweak, we may now say that, for example, Mars in Leo in the third house rules Venus in Scorpio in the sixth, and *all of it* will be based on the *simple influences* of the planets Venus and Mars, *as they interact with the hexagonal crystal at the center of the Earth*. We no longer need starry constellations whatsoever.

It is when we take astrology *out* of the sky and put it *in* the Earth and *on* the Earth that we realize astrology's staggering power and its incredible capacity for detail. We no longer hesitate how astrology's mysterious, invisible influences can be transferred from one side of an empty sky to another, equally empty sky, seemingly on mere whim. We are instead witnesses to the inner dynamics of the Earth's own crystalline structure.

These on-going planets-to-crystal relationships are complemented by **special relationships**, known as *aspects*, which occur when the planets form harmonics between each other, as seen from the Earth and as framed and defined by the Earth's central crystal. When two planets form an exact aspect they create a vibration *external* to the Earth itself, but one which *strongly impacts the Earth*, by means of *vibratory sympathy with the Earth's central hexagonal crystal*. Blinded by the sky, intimidated by a phony science, modern astrologers have been guilty of over-emphasizing aspects, at the expense of the Earth's more powerful, underlying astrological forces.

The various external planetary influences combine to change the vibratory rate of the Earth's central crystal, from moment to moment. The understanding and use of Astrology is obvious, logical, and necessary to all life on this planet.

George McCormack

We have now arrived at an understanding of McCormack's astonishing finding, that planets exactly on the midheaven/immum coeli (MC/IC, 10th/4th) have the strongest impact upon the Earth's weather. Consider that a planet placed on the IC will not only be passing its resonant energies directly *through* the Earth itself, but these energies, combined, enhanced and amplified by *precise alignment to the underlying crystalline energies of the Earth itself*, will emerge from the ground at *right angles to the surface*. In other words, with *maximum combined force*.

I remember an old rule from alchemy. The alchemical process, which is scoffed at by many, was said to require total darkness, or moonlight, in order to succeed. Moonlight is not merely very weak light, it is also *polarized*. Which is to say, light reflected over a great distance is polarized merely by the combination of reflection and distance.

If the Sun and planets (presumably also including the Earth's Moon) are crystalline structures, then the harmonic resonances that pass between them are presumably *polarized* as well. When these resonances arrive and then meet with the Earth in a precise polarity (the MC/IC axis), polarized-polarized results would be expected. McCormack terms this "magnetic action" (pg. 92 and elsewhere). I would refine this and call it *magnetic polarization*.

Planets are not magnetic to each other *per se*. They *become magnetic* when, in the sky, they are polarized at specific hexagonal angles. While holding those angles, they have specific impact upon the Earth's central crystal and its various discreet energies. Which that crystal then radiates in a general fashion to the planet as a whole, affecting all that live and breathe and crawl on its surface, and, specifically, radiates to key locations which affect the atmosphere and weather locally, if not mundane events as well. Precisely as McCormack describes.

McCormack notes that planets that make 90° aspects to the MC/IC axis are themselves powerful. Which they should be. But note what he did *not* say: With the exception of the Moon, McCormack rarely bothers with the ascendant/descendant. Was this an oversight on his part?

No. Fairlawn, New Jersey, where McCormack made his observations, is 41° north of the Equator. At that latitude, the ascendant/descendant axis is rarely at right angles to the MC/IC. In terms of astrometeorology, McCormack did not find the Asc/Dsc angles to be of importance. Instead, he found the raw 90° angle itself to be supreme. This is a most important detail. McCormack is *not* describing astrology per se. He is, for the most part, describing the *astrology of the atmosphere*. The atmosphere is the part of the Earth with the least mass, it therefore has the least *resonance*. In practical terms, there may very well not be enough mass in the atmosphere for rulerships to apply.

In this regard I am reminded of the work of John H. Nelson (1903-1984). From the 1940's to his retirement in 1971, Nelson was employed by RCA in New York to identify and forecast times of radio interference. He quickly identified specific planet to planet *heliocentric* aspects as the culprits, eventually achieving a high degree of forecast accuracy. Why heliocentric? Consider that radio waves are broadcast from towers high above the Earth's surface, radiate into space itself and are presumably directly influenced by solar and planetary energies. Lacking all earthly matter, the Earth's own astrology would not seem to apply to radio transmission at all. It is very likely that Nelson and McCormack knew each other. I would very much like to know their opinion of each others' work, but I digress.

In studying McCormack's work, I gather that in the process of deducing that high and low pressure areas involve exchanges in the levels of the atmosphere, he was first drawn to highland and lowland areas as where these exchanges would be most clearly felt. He then presumably extended his observations to waterways and finally to sandy soil. In the process he stumbled upon something else of extraordinary interest.

It seems he accidentally hit upon a connection between western astrometeorology and Chinese Feng Shui. The term "Feng Shui" translates as "wind/water." It is the Chinese system of landscape management. It is also directly tied to Chinese astrology.

Chinese astrology is different from Western astrology, or, for that matter, Vedic astrology or Persian astrology, and this is because of number.

For many centuries astrology remained in the tropics, principally in India.

Alexandria, at 32° N, was a lonely outpost. The reason was because astrology needs a house system in order to best express itself, and house systems are the simplest and work best in tropical latitudes, where houses and signs tend to overlap. Leave the tropics and the two systems diverge. By the time you reach northern Europe—or central China (Beijing is 40°N)—simple equal houses will not work, nor will trisections in zodiacal longitude (Porphyry) work. A proper house system trisects the Prime Vertical, either in space, or by time.

To do this handily, you must have a sophisticated number system, which the ancients lacked. Instead, they had hash-marks, the best of which seems to have been the Roman system (I, II, III, IV, etc.). Complex computations with hashmarks are not impossible, but they are unwieldy, which is why many ancient peoples employed the abacus to do sums.

Starting around 300 AD, India developed a number system based on place values, which we now call Arabic numbers. These were adopted by the Arabs in the 9th century, and in 1202 were introduced to Europe by Fibonacci. This single event revolutionized all Europe, but, regrettably China was left out. China did not adapt Arabic numbers until the 20th century.

To this day China has a variety of crude number systems, which is why it retained the abacus centuries after it had been abandoned elsewhere. China was too far north to equate houses with signs, so, lacking numbers, China was unable to erect astrological charts. Instead, they developed an entirely different system of astrology, one based on the 60 year cycles of Saturn and Jupiter. (From which, by the way, they get their five elements: Jupiter's cycle is 12 years, it makes five cycles in 60 years, while Saturn makes two.) By this reasoning, Feng Shui is the expression of the Earth's raw Zodiacal sign energies as they directly manifest in the environment. The combination of a crystalline Earth-based system of astrology, George McCormack's astrometeorology, and Feng Shui, may produce surprising results.

Astrology is under our feet. It radiates from the ground up. We are soaked in it, always have been, and always will be. We can no more deny it, than we can deny gravity.

And with that, I give you this extraordinary book. Enjoy!

David R. Roell
Bel Air, MD
April 18, 2012

Charts in this book are calculated with the Mean Node, Placidus houses, and day/night Part of Fortune. Note that McCormack does not use Fortuna, did not place Pluto in his charts, and except where noted, did not specify latitude. I have presumed 40°
N. — *Editor.*

ASTRO-METEOROLGY

There has been an urgent demand for a modern textbook on the theory and practice of astro-meteorology, based on exhaustive studies and critical tests of all astral principles concerned. Herein is presented a private course of comprehensive instructions based on 40 years of practical experience in astral principles and more than 33 years of diligent studies and observations applied to long range weather forecasting.

These rules were critically tested in a series of articles published in <u>Azoth</u> Magazine (New York) in 1917-18 when the coldest temperatures on record—13 degrees below zero on December 30, 1917—and the record maximum temperature of 102.6, on August 6, 1918, were forecast fully three months in advance. Similar tests in three series of long range detailed forecasts for thirty consecutive days as published in the New York <u>World</u> in 1925-26, periodical long range weather forecasts in the Student-Adept, those of the Mississippi and Missouri River floods, published in Wynn's <u>Astrology</u> Magazine, April, 1944 and others in the monthly <u>Bulletin</u> of the American Federation of Astrologers attest to the rationality of this scientific methods of long range weather forecasting for long periods ahead, for any part of the world, based on astronomical calculations.

Voluminous chart data, accompanied by supporting weather records, with each lesson, elucidate the principles presented and furnish unequivocal testimonies to support the validity of this modern system.

Every paragraph embodies a rule. Each paragraph is indexed for ready reference in either individual or class instruction.

This work, which we believe is the most comprehensive yet published on the subject, reveals new methods of determining the geographical origin of various atmospheric phenomena and timing weather to any required longitude. These methods are further refined with a view toward proving the astronomic causes of seismic phenomena, epidemics, anomalous weather and cycles, together with progressive studies pertaining to the Moon's Nodes.

The author is indebted to Pearce'e <u>Textbook of Astrology</u>, the late John Hazelrigg, eminent American astrologer, and the United States Weather Bureau, from which sources valuable assistance and inspiration have been received in pursuing these researches. Grateful thanks is also expressed to fellow members and students of the A.F.A. who have generously collaborated in collecting and forwarding records of weather phenomena.

GEORGE J. McCORMACK
Fair Lawn, New Jersey, U.S.A.

ASTRO-METEOROLOGY

GUIDE TO LONG RANGE WEATHER FORECASTING
by George J. McCormack

The study of astro-meteorology, of the influence of the heavenly bodies upon the weather, dates back to remotest antiquity. By this system, the ancients were skilled not only in predicting the general character of the weather for <u>seasons</u>, but also in prognosticating earthquakes, epidemics, the periods of famine and plenty, of prolonged drought, dampness, heat or excessive cold for seasons involved.

Since those ancient times, religions, orthodox scientific beliefs have changed time and again, but the fundamental rules for predicting weather as handed down to posterity by Claudius Ptolemy, in his <u>Tetrabiblos</u> eighteen centuries ago, are still used by astro-meteorologists without requiring alteration.

In our opinion, based on more than twenty-six years of specialized researches in connection with astro-meteorology, we are convinced that to abandon this research is to render the discovery of the laws which regulate the weather, hopeless. The federal meteorologists, by plotting daily weather maps and depending on mechanical devices for determining barometric pressure, temperature and humidity variations, velocities and directions of wind, etc. can venture fairly reliable forecasts of the weather 24 hours in advance. Beyond that period, official weather forecasters are dealing with uncertainties and confining weather forecasts mostly to prudent guesses.

Observations of sunspots alone will never lead to the discovery

1

of the laws which regulate the weather. The atmosphere is often liable to unusual and long continued impressions, and these are induced by planetary action on the earth as well as on the Sun. Astro-meteorological researches covering many years have indicated that the maximum frequency of sunspots coincide with the perihelion passage of Jupiter at cycles of 11.86 years, when positive electricity in the atmosphere is at a maximum, excessive drought coincides with the phenomena and the rate of mortality is also low. The minimum frequency of sunspots half way between these periods of Jupiter's perihelion are observed to follow a similar cycle of 11.9 years, at which periods negative electricity reaches a maximum in the atmosphere, an increase in the mortality is noted and great frost ensue. The record cold wave of February 9, 1934 when temperatures at Washington, D.C. dropped to 14 degrees below zero, was an instance indicating how attendant phenomena can accentuate and intensify either heat or cold. On the day previous the Sun had formed a conjunction with Saturn in the cold-crystallizing sign Aquarius while <u>Jupiter was in aphelion</u>.

Yet strange as it may seem, W.R. Gregg, who was then Chief of the U.S. Weather Bureau, reported that on February 9,1934, when the temperature fell to 14 below zero, the intensity of radiation received from the Sun was the greatest ever recorded in Washington! Astrometeorologists do not have to seek far for the answer to that paradox.

Every astro-meteorologist believes and knows, that when planets form certain angles with the Sun and earth, certain known influences are the result. These influences appear to arise from the light reflected from each planet into our atmosphere, which light acts chemically or electrically, according to its nature. For instance, Mars reflects the <u>red</u> ray of light. It is a well attested fact that <u>light</u> and <u>heat</u> both exist in the atmosphere and that the latter is but a modification of the former. It is also a well attested fact that the component parts of the atmosphere—when brought in contact in given proportions, and fired by the electric spark, produce perfect light; and also that <u>oxygen</u>, the <u>red ray</u> of solar light, and <u>positive electricity</u> are identical, and that the <u>blue ray</u> of light, or <u>nitrogen</u> is equivalent to <u>negative electricity</u>.

The planets Saturn and Uranus reflect the blue ray, negative electricity and induce <u>descending</u> air currents. Uranus reflecting the actinic rays at the negative side of the solar spectrum, operates with more sudden intensity and from higher atmospheric stratas.

Hence, regardless of the intensity of radiation where the Sun's rays contact the earth's surface, it is the descending air currents from upper stratas of the atmosphere that bring down the cold. Coincidentally, the winds blow down slope, giving the impression that they originate in the Arctic.

Conversely the planet Mars reflects the red ray, positive electricity and ascending air currents, accordingly facilitating solar radiation, promoting heat and drought and consequently increasing fire hazards. But when mixed with rays of contrary nature, the rays reflected by this planet can produce turbulence. Venus operates to produce milder temperatures, with accompanying humidity and temperate showers, seldom with strong winds. Jupiter conduces to increase of oxygen and in combination with Mars effects thunder storms even in mid-winter, in places where the combined bodies hold relative geometrical angles to the earth. Mercury is neutral, reflecting the nature of planets with which it may be in configuration, but has a potential effect on directions of wind and their velocity. Neptune effects freak weather through extremely sudden changes that may range from humid calms or cold weather fogs to devastating hurricanes or floods. Characterized by vertical ascending air currents, charged with moisture, Neptune conduces to vacuums and its effects are intensified over small areas at a time. We are not prepared, as yet, to reach conclusive findings regarding the planet Pluto's relation to weather.

0.01—<u>MAJOR STATIONS OF PLANETS</u>:
    When planets are occupying major stations, their general characteristics are strongly impressed on the weather progressively around the globe. In this respect the slower moving planets exert their influences on weather intermittently for weeks and even months. These stations are as follows:

(a) In perigee, i.e., closest to the earth.
(b) In Perihelion, i.e., when at their nearest point to the Sun.
(c) In apogee, i.e. , farthest distance from the earth.
(d) In Aphelion, i.e., at their greatest distance, from the Sun.
(e) In addition to these, the periods of 9½ years when the Moon's North Node arrives at the equinoctial points, coinciding with the Moon's greatest or least extreme north declination. (Observed to affect ocean currents and induce cyclic climatic abnormalities.)

The foregoing may be overlooked in initial studies, since they are related to more technical applications as later referred to in our analyses. Of more frequent occurrence and allowing for continued practical study are the following positions of major importance:

(f) In the Equator ($0°00"$ declination).

(g) When occupying the Tropics, particularly North Tropic (extreme north declination).

(h) Eclipses of the Sun or Moon. Conjunctions of the major planets.

0.02—ASPECTS OR MAGNETIC ANGLES:

If asked why there should be any force, virtue, or potency in these particular angles (all multiples of 15 degrees being magnetic and varying in power of intensity) that should cause effects, either on the temperature or any other state of the atmosphere, to appear when the heavenly bodies form among themselves these particular angles, we may say that these geometric angles demonstrate both positive and negative electro-magnetic virtues. The earth reacts to these angles or to planets in outer space similarly as a radio dial being rotated to a certain wave length will tune in a radio station.

The "aspects" or configurations observed to be most effective in meteorology are the following differences in longitude as given under three classifications for future reference.

(A) - Aspects under class A incline to fair weather, affect temperatures and wind velocity principally, and with relative powers in the order given are $60°$, $120°$, $30°$, and $150°$.

(B) - Configurations under class B are normally disturbing to the atmosphere, especially when bodies of contrary nature are combined. Both atmospheric moisture and temperatures are affected. With power in the order given, these are $180°$, 90, $45°$, and $135°$.

(C) - In class C we include the conjunction and the parallel of declination as neutral configurations. When heavenly bodies of contrary nature are combined under these configurations, changes of winds and distribution of atmospheric pressure are conducive to atmospheric disturbance. (Refer to Table 0.04, Sun's configurations with the various planets.)

0.03—GENERAL INFLUENCE OF PLANETS WHEN STATIONARY, OR IN THE EQUATOR OR TROPICS.

♆ **NEPTUNE** usually conduces to variable "freak" weather, lowering barometer, southerly winds, humidity, excessive static, hazes, fogs, sudden changes, more effectively in lowlands and along waterways. Combined with Mars, this planet is related to seismic phenomena.

Spring: Misty and mild. Fogs at night. Sudden changes.
Summer: Sultry; warm. If thick haze, sudden showers.
Autumn: Lower barometer. Mild; misty. Showers at night
Winter: Damp and foggy. Vertical ascending currents. Unsettled.

♅ Keynote of **URANUS** is high barometric pressure, descending vertical air currents, increased wind velocity and sudden changes to colder. Winds are <u>gusty</u>. Sudden frosts and cold snaps. Affects highlands first, then downslope.

Spring: Overcast, cold and blustery. Chilly drizzles. Frosts at night.
Summer: Winds shifting to N.W. Storms originate in highlands then south. Temperature falls.
Autumn: Gusty. Chilly. Bleak skies. Fine rain. Often cold drizzle. Frosts.
Winter: Windy and stormy. Fresh to strong N.W. winds. Cold wave follows.

♄ **SATURN's** keynote is lowering barometer, steady but decisively. Shadows, dampness and cold. Easterly winds. Effects very general over large areas. Low hanging clouds. Excessive humidity, slow build up of low pressure areas with increasing cloudiness. Downfall under this planet is more lasting than with any other.

Spring: Increasing cloudiness. Damp and wet. Colder.
Summer: Overcast, humid, showery then colder.
Autumn: Low clouds. North Easters. Rain and colder.
Winter: Increasing cloudiness. Stormy. Colder.

♂ **MARS's** keynote is sharp, quick action, with normal tendency to evaporation. General influence is calorific, inducing elevation of temperature, drought. Westerly winds. Hottest when in the sign Leo. When in B or C aspects with Saturn, Uranus, Mercury, it is inflammatory; when with Venus "makes her cry" when with Jupiter induces heat waves, thunder; when with

Neptune, squalls and seismic phenomena. In water signs, more conducive to brief storms.

Spring: Dry air, Moderate temperature
Summer: Heat waves. Local thunder storms at night along waterways.
Autumn: Warmer temperatures. Thunder.
Winter: Warmer. Changes to unsettled.

♀ The influence of **VENUS** is mild. South winds prevail and velocity is comparatively moderate. This planet is the rain and snow maker par excellence and has dominion over the April rains. Sloppiest when occupying the sign Scorpio. Flood maker with Neptune. Temperature rises and humidity is excessive under the Venus influence.

Spring: Excessive humidity. Warm south winds. Showers, highlands to lowlands. Then cooler.
Summer: In North Tropic, warm and sultry. In equator, particularly (Aries) showery.
Autumn: South winds. Humid. Rainy then colder.
Winter: South winds. Snow or rain. Then colder.

☿ The key note of **MERCURY** is wind. Alone neutral, this planet reflects the character of planets to which it forms aspects. The positions in the equator (0°00' Declination) are important.

Spring: Windy and variable.
Summer: Breezy and variable.
Autumn: Colder rainy and windy.
Winter: Stormy, with rain or snow. Colder.

0.04—THE SUN CONFIGURED WITH THE VARIOUS PLANETS, AND THEIR GENERAL INFLUENCE ON THE ATMOSPHERE.

☉ — ☿ Sun and MERCURY

Spring: (A) Generally fair and windy.
(B, C) Rain and strong winds. Retrograde Mercury wind and gales.

Summer: (A) Fair, breezy, cooler.
(B, C) Breezy, variable. Generally showery.

Autumn: (A) Generally windy and fair.
(B, C) Rain and wind followed by colder night.

Winter: (A) Fair, windy, and colder.
(B, C) High wind velocity. Retrograde Mercury often blizzards.

☉ — ♀ Sun and VENUS

Spring: (A) Rising temperature. Brilliant atmosphere.
(B, C) Warm and humid, followed by showers.

Summer: (A) Warm and misty. Fine weather.
(B, C) Hot and sultry, followed by dashing showers.

Autumn: (A) Clear and mild.
(B, C) Increasing cloudiness, rain and colder.

Winter: (A) Fair and milder.
(B, C) Fog and much rain. Colder.

☉ — ♂ Sun and MARS

Spring: (A) Evaporation. Warmer.
(B, C) Warmer but unsettled.

Summer: (A) Heat and rapid evaporation. Note conjunction and 60 degree aspects particularly, for heat.
(B, C) Heat and static. Thunderstorms in lowlands.

Autumn: (A) Sudden rises in temperature. Dry.
(B, C) Warm and dry atmosphere.

Winter: (A) Clear, with moderately high temperatures.
(B, C) Fair, milder. Increased solar radiation.

☉ — ♃ Sun and JUPITER

The conjunction, Parallel and 60 degree aspects, rising temperature.

Spring: (A) Fine growing weather. Winds North.
(B) Mild, pleasant.

Summer: (A) Hot but plenitude of ozone. Generally fine.
(B) Warmer. Local thunderstorms.

Autumn: (A) Moderate, pleasant breezes.
(B) Moderate, breezy.

Winter: (A) Warmer and pleasant.
(B) Mild and breezy.

☉ — ♄ Sun and SATURN

Spring: (A) Partly cloudy and colder. Night frosts in highlands.
(B) Lower barometer. Dull to overcast skies. EASTERLY WINDS. Heavy downfall, colder.

Summer: (A) Local showers, followed by cool and moderately breezy.
(B) East winds. Slowly falling barometer. Intense, general rains. Hail or thunder. Cooler.

Autumn: (A) Partly cloudy. Cooler. Frosty nights, highlands.
(B) East to North East winds. Cold and stormy. Thick low clouds. Colder.

Winter: (A) Fair and colder, particularly in the interior.
(B) Northeasters. Rain, snow, heavy, followed by cold wave.

Parallel of declination induces lower temperatures as under (A) except when one declination is north and the other planet is south or vice versa.

Conjunction usually operates under (B)

☉ — ♅ Sun and URANUS

Spring: (A) Descending air currents. Fair and colder. Gusty winds. CRISIS WEATHER.
(B) Bleak atmosphere. Storms range southward. Very chilly rains. Erratic winds.

Summer: (A) Fair, breezy and North West winds from interior; quick rising barometer. Much cooler.

(B) Overcast, squally. Sudden changes to cooler. Damp and penetrating.

Autumn: (A) North West winds. Downslope. Fair, windy and colder. Cold waves in interior. Night frosts.
(B) Damp, windy and often accompanied by prolonged drizzles. Much colder, interior. Night frosts.

Winter: (A) Fresh to strong North West winds. High barometer. Sudden cold waves. Heavy frosts.
(B) Cold and damp. Increasing wind velocity. Sleet or snow. Then cold wave.

(C) Abnormally high barometer, sudden declines of temperature, accompanied by vertically descending winds from higher atmospheric strata and downslope. Usually North West winds prevail. Note absence of clouds in the sky. Yet this clear weather disfavors skywriters.

☉ — ♆ Sun and NEPTUNE

Spring: (A) Conduces to ASCENDING AIR CURRENTS. Mild and pleasant air. South to South West wind. Shifting moderate breezes, rising temperature.
(B) Calm but misty. Sudden changes. Foggy in highlands.

Summer: (A) Fair and warm, but breezy. Usually good sailing weather.

(B) Hot and sultry. Sudden local squalls in lowlands, following narrow paths. No relief from heat. Unfavorable for small sailing craft.

Autumn: (A) Mild and pleasant. Rising temperature. Sometimes misty. Lows pass over more northerly course. Warm in lowlands.
(B) Windy and rainy in lowlands. Fogs in highlands. Temperatures rise.

Winter: (A) Rising temperatures. Low velocity of wind. Generally pleasant atmosphere.
(B) Stormy and foggy. Heavy smoke fog in large cities. Downfall heavy, usually rain. Shifting winds.

(C) Temperature rises. Mist is principal feature. Freak weather, changing suddenly from one extreme to another. Ascending air currents. Both (B) and (C) configurations present difficulties for air navigation at low altitudes.

Effects of solar configurations, tracing paths eastward, will arrive at a point of observation in one to three days. Details for definite timing by charts will appear later in this series.

Each planet, though representing the embodiment of a principle in the atmosphere, registers a dual quality of influence dependent on whether it forms harmonious (A) or inharmonious (B) configurations with other bodies or magnetic angles to the place of observation. The type of aspect operating should always be duly considered. The influences of planets also vary according to the nature of the signs which they may occupy. Again, if one planet of hot and fiery nature, like Mars, should form a conjunction, square or opposition with a cold planet like Saturn or Uranus, it would be only reasonable to expect that atmospheric disturbances would result at some specific point in geographic longitude where both bodies were holding magnetic angles to the Earth. The low pressure area, thus originated, proceeds on an easterly course, varying in character as it passes over various points in longitude eastward. Since weather conditions in one particular area will influence winds and the distribution of moisture in adjacent areas, the direction of winds is among other important factors in weather prognoses. The directions of winds frequently indicate the positions of high pressure areas or the centers of low barometric pressure areas in relation to the point of observation. Before we proceed with discussion of these details, let us first consider the fundamental principles of the planetary bodies as related to weather.

G-1—MERCURY.

Mercury relates to the violet ray in the solar spectrum and is associated with wind pressure. Never more than twenty-eight degrees distant in longitude from the Sun, this symbolic "Winged Messenger" can only form the conjunction and parallel of declination with the solar orb. Ordinarily, Mercury reflects the quality of the sign in which it is tenanted. At periods when this body is at its greatest elongation from the Sun, when apparently retrograde and conjunction with the Sun, when apparently stationary, or when occupying either the Equator or North Tropic, there is a general tendency to excite the velocity of the winds to a marked degree. Geographic areas where Mercury occupies the angles, principally the 4th or 10th houses of ingress or lunation maps, should be carefully considered in this respect.

Of variable nature, Mercury's influence on winds and consequent atmospheric conditions depends not only on planets with which it may be configured but also the character of the angles thus formed. Favorable (A) aspects may be indicative of breezes from certain points of the compass with resultant effects on temperature, but with accompanying fair weather. Unfavorable configurations (B)—sometimes also (C)—such as oppositions, squares or conjunctions (Sun, Mars, Saturn or Uranus), on the other hand stir up conflicting cross currents in the various atmospheric stratas that will subsequently excite atmospheric turbulence, especially if Mercury combines its influence with two or more planets which may then be forming storm breeding aspects.

Owing to Mercury's rapid motion and its higher frequency of configurations, this celestial arbiter "monkeys" with our weather through its well attested influence relating to the direction and velocity of winds. We have gathered voluminous statistical data over a period of many years concerning extremes of weather coinciding with important configurations of Mercury. These records include specific localities and dates and substantiate traditional rules concerning this planet's effectiveness in producing high wind pressure. Numerous hurricanes originating in the West Indies or the Caribbean Sea have coincided with Mercury's conjunction or opposition with Uranus during early spring or late summer months respectively. Some of the most destructive sleet storms and blizzards in winter and cold months have been characterized by Mercury in the lower meridian and forming a conjunction, opposition or even a sextile angle with Uranus. Records also indicate that highest barometric pressure and wind velocity, with accompanying sharp declines of temperatures, have culminated under the combined Mercury-Uranus influences. When these two bodies are forming the aforesaid configurations, they are truly the "electrical planets par excellence" and can play havoc with transportation, highway traffic and overhead communication lines. An illustration was October 28, 1938.

Winds normally induced by Mercury's aspects with other planets are as follows. With **VENUS**, southerly winds with resultant warmer temperatures. Low pressure areas veer to the northward. With **MARS**, westerly winds, seasonal temperatures in winter and cool seasons. In summer, hot and dry, with reddish clouds. Atmosphere depends largely on nature of the signs tenanted by Mars. Sudden changes, with high velocity winds and thunderstorms often develop, particularly if the Moon be in perigee at the same time. With **JUPITER**, northerly winds, wool packed clouds, fair weather moderate wind velocity and temperature. With **SATURN**, lower barometer, easterly winds, increasing humidity and variable degrees of cloudiness which may range to overcast skies. With **URANUS**, increasing velocity of winds from northwest, rising barometer, accompanied by lower ranges of temperature. Winds, according to positions and aspects may range from fresh winds to gale force. During periods of heat in warm seasons, these configurations induce severe storms, particularly in the highlands, the winds being spasmodic, in gusts and descending from higher atmospheric stratas. During very cold seasons Mercury-Uranus conjunctions, oppositions, squares or stationary positions, or when combined with Venus or Mars, are potential blizzard breeders. Invariably, they are troublesome for all means of traffic and overland communication lines.

G-2—VENUS:

♀ Venus symbolizes the yellow ray in the solar spectrum, conduces to winds from the south with accompanying rising temperatures south to north as low barometric pressure areas veer northward and attract winds to their centers. Representing the copper element in Nature's batteries, this planet, like Neptune, is powerfully magnetic and is one of the chief agents in the perturbation of the earth, in her orbital motion. The keynote of Venus is humidity and warmth and its general tendency weatherwise is to make moisture pregnant. Breezes under the Venus influence are usually gentle, but the winds from the south increase humidity and cause the temperature to rise. Temperate showers are normally characterized by this planet. Venus is very sensitive to configurations with other planets and downfall is observed to be excessive when conjunctions, oppositions, squares or parallels of declination are formed with <u>Sun</u>, <u>Neptune</u> (downpours), <u>Saturn</u> (prolonged northeasters, or drizzles if Venus occupies cold signs). With <u>Mars</u>, warmer temperatures, followed by dashing rains are observed. Cooler weather usually follows showers under the Venus signature, particularly when the planets Saturn or Uranus are concerned. Visibility then improves appreciably. Venus-Uranus combinations generally incline to high barometric pressure, sometimes to an abnormal degree. The 60 degree angle between these bodies induces a cloudless sky, brilliant sunshine, with accompanying minimum wind velocity—a perfect blend for outdoor photography or sky writing.

As Venus' arc of greatest elongation from the Sun is never more than 48 degrees, it follows that besides the conjunction and parallel of declination the only aspect of any force which she can form with the Sun is the angle of 45 degrees. The angle of 30 degrees is usually considered of minor importance in weather prognosis. Since the 45 degree angle from the Sun falls close to the angle of greatest elongation, heaviest precipitation frequently ensues under this aspect, and more so if Venus then occupy either Taurus, Cancer, Scorpio or Pisces.

When in the Equator (0.00 declination), in the North Tropic (extreme north declination), apparently stationary, or when conjunction with the Sun in moist signs or in Taurus, and particularly if then retrograde, Venus exerts a temperate and wet influence and has relatively greater potency for general downfall in the lowlands. When combined with Uranus, the interior is more generally responsive to cold waves, slow, cold drizzles, with accompanying winds moving downslope. In the colder seasons, the planet Venus can produce heaviest snowfalls in the shortest periods of time. Owing to the prevailing south winds, humidity and moisture builds up as the barometer falls and the atmosphere becomes charged with mist. A peculiar calm precedes winter snow storms under this planet's configurations, with a mist in high air stratas screening the Sun.

When Venus occupies the lower meridian of an ingress or lunation chart, downfall in excess is indicated for the period involved and such reach maximum over the interior. Southerly winds should preponderate and temperatures above the normal average may be expected unless Venus is near extreme south declination. In late

Autumn, early Spring and during Winter months, this signature predicates heavy snows over northern parts. Over southern parts, from the nadir position of Venus and eastward, expect milder weather with accompanying downfall. If tenanting the upper meridian (10th house), then interpret excessive downfall over the southern areas, with cold waves from the interior immediately following the storms. The 3rd and 9th houses should be duly considered as similarly affecting geographical areas immediately westward of the observation point. These atmospheric conditions then develop eastward. Thus can be appreciated the reason why weather conditions in one area are related to and dependent upon atmospheric phenomena in adjacent areas. Local atmospheric changes are more frequent in warm seasons than during winter months and are responsive to geodetic and topographical considerations which we will discuss later in this treatise.

Venus is responsive not only to the particular nature of the sign it occupies but also to planets with which it may form aspects. Negative in nature, this planet operates to an appreciable extent as a conductor of <u>moisture</u> and of magnetic currents similarly as a copper wire conducts radio waves and impulses. Under the harmonious (A) configurations this heavenly body promises delightful sunshine, but such aspects to Saturn or Uranus indicate lower temperatures.

G-3—<u>MARS</u>:

The keynote of Mars is energy, heat and dryness. But when mixed with storm indicating elements, this planetary body induces turbulence and destruction weatherwise. When considered alone, it relates to heat and drought, both of which are accentuated when Mars is in perigee (closest to the earth in its orbital motion), when in extreme north declination and when occupying the lower meridian in an ingress, eclipse or lunation chart. As the sidereal period of Mars is 1.881 years, this planet's orbital motion relates to the periodic fluctuations in outbreaks of <u>martial</u> or inflammatory and feverish ailments. Statistical analysis by insurance companies would very likely reveal a 19 year cycle in connection with outbreaks of smallpox, though such epidemics would each time affect a different geographic area. And it might be further observed that these periodic cycles of pandemic martial diseases relate closely to prolonged droughts affecting the geographic areas concerned. We will refer to this subject in detail under G-9 at the conclusion of our series.

Under the Mars influence, temperatures range above the normal average. Effects of this planet on weather when it occupies the equator, the North Tropic, also when it forms a conjunction or 60 degree angle with the Sun, invariably attest to its ascribed influence on the atmosphere. It signifies the west wind and evaporation. Greatest heat prevails where Mars occupies the sign Leo at an ingress or lunation and tenants the meridian, meanwhile configured with Sun or Jupiter. The conjunction of Mars and Venus impregnates the air with moisture along waterways. Preceded by rising temperatures, the low pressure areas sweep over the lowlands and culminate in heavy downfall, but without thunder even in summer. Never a drizzle under this combination. All aspects between Mars and Venus incline to elevation of temperature accompanied by minimum breeze, but not all configurations between these two bodies will promise showers. Dr. Goad's expressed belief that the conjunction and opposition of the Sun with Mars disturbs the ocean currents appears to have been supported by exhaustive observations. Under Sun-Mars configurations, the more intense the heat, the greater the atmospheric turbulence to follow when the heat wave breaks. Mars storms usually develop from west to east, preceded by a strong wind. In summer, excessive radio static heralds the approaching thunderstorm.

A discordant Mars is exciting and ever indicative of friction. In weather, Mars induces this friction by atmospheric turbulence. One of the peculiarities of the planet Mars, as well attested by prolonged observations, is that, when adversely affecting a particular point, it invariably leaves its mark. This may result from thunderstorms, spontaneous combustion or fires during spells of excessive heat or drought, or destructive winds when combined with Mercury, Saturn or Uranus.

An interesting chart demonstrating the potential influence of Mars when on the lower meridian at a solar ingress was that for the Winter Solstice, December 21, 1936, 7:18 p.m., L.M.T., Washington, D.C., in which the midheaven was Aries 21.00 and the Ascendant was Leo 3.37. Mars was posited in Libra 21.47 and exactly on the lower meridian at Washington, D.C. This nadir position predicated a higher range of temperatures than normal for the season. Our published forecast to this effect, as early as September, 1936, was amply verified by the open winter of 1936-37 along the Atlantic Seaboard.

G-4—JUPITER:

The keynote of Jupiter is expansion and purification. Northerly winds of moderate velocity and fine weather cumuli clouds generally prevail under the normal action of Jupiter. A maximum generation of ozone accompanies high barometric pressure. Although Jupiter is commonly associated with thunder, the influence of this planet tends to reduce static electricity. Storms arising from Jupiter's magnetic positions or configurations are usually followed by a clear, fresh condition of the atmosphere, even in hottest periods. This planet may reasonably be termed the "air-conditioner" of the atmosphere. It's action combines temperate moisture with heat.

It is quite probable that Jupiter, because of its ponderousness, exerts a strong magnetic pull on the earth as well as on other bodies and that it affects terrestrial magnetism appreciably. When occupying fixed signs, principally Taurus and Aquarius, this planet exerts a more "fixed" pull on the earth's crust. Seismic disturbances have been observed to increase in intensity during such periods. When Jupiter tenants the sign Scorpio, volcanic activity, coinciding with the explosive nature of Scorpio, frequently results. Some details of these manifestations together with periods of magnetic displays, as recorded in our past observations, will be reviewed in statistical data under Jupiter.

Although normally inclining to moderately higher temperatures for the season, Jupiter's influence on weather may vary according to its combinations with other bodies. Jupiter and Mars are conducive to excessive heat, drought, sudden but brief spells of static. In warm seasons the subsequent thunder storms clarify the atmosphere. Under this combination, thunder sometimes manifests even in mid-winter. An interesting example of Jupiter's effect on seasonal temperatures was its nadir position in the thermal sign Leo at the Winter Solstice in December, 1931 (December 22, 2:22 p.m. L.M.T., Washington. D.C.) which accounted for the abnormally mild winter that followed along the Atlantic Seaboard.

When Jupiter is in conjunction with the Sun or forming angles of 60 degrees or 120 degrees thereto, northerly winds of moderate velocity, wool-packed fleecy clouds, clear visibility and "growing weather" are indicated. Displays of the Aurora Borealis are more frequent and brilliant when Uranus and Jupiter are conjoined, as on May 7, 1941, or when in opposition or square to each other. Abnormally high wind pressure times very closely to these phenomena and magnetic storms disrupt both radio and wire communications service.   If the United States Weather Bureau will review weather records over a period of years on dates when the configurations were formed, particularly concerning the conjunctions and oppositions of these two major bodies, the results should be self-explanatory and yield unequivocal evidence that the combined action of these two planets is responsible for the magnetic storm cold waves and gales of cold wind flowing down from very high air stratas.

0-5—SATURN:

ħ The keynote of Saturn is concentration. Although the positive influence of this heavenly body relates to crystallization, cold and humidity, and its negative positions and configurations are conducive to condensation of aqueous vapors, prevailing easterly winds, heavy low clouds and slow but decisive lowering barometer, it concentrates the influence of the sign in which it may be tenanted. When transiting the winter signs, near extreme south declination, its potency for cold increases. When occupying major stations, i.e. in perihelion, when nearest to the earth (perigee), or when in the Equator, North Tropic, also when stationary, east winds predominate. These winds are contrary to the normal rotation of the earth from west to east on its axis. The barometer then falls, accompanied by increasing cloudiness and downfall.

The negative influence of Saturn is likewise impressed on the atmosphere when this body occupies the lower meridian at a place of observation, or when forming conjunction or "B" angles with significators of positive electrical nature. Humidity is usually featured under Saturn's negative influence and the air is depressive during hot as well as cold, stormy weather. Dampness prevails more in the lowlands but Saturn engenders more cold under the same aspects over the higher altitudes of the interior. This planet imparts negative electricity in the atmosphere and the weather changes induced are slow in developing, broad in scope and slow in clearing up. They do not operate everywhere exactly at the culmination of an aspect but can be definitely timed from a geographic point where Saturn occupies the meridian of the solar ingress chart for the quarter.

Under positive ("A") aspects, particularly sextile (60°) angles, this planet is indicative of fair weather, but with appreciable decline in temperatures.

Since the sidereal period of Saturn is 29.46 years and it remains in each sign for approximately two and a half years, it's influence is gradual and prolonged. Thus, when occupying major stations, the effects of Saturn may recur intermittently to produce abnormal weather conditions throughout an entire season. For illustration, when Saturn occupied the North Tropic in 1915 (as will also be indicated during the summer of 1944) the summer season at New York was observed to be damp and cloudy, with accompanying excessive downfall, thus predicating an unfavorable and unprofitable season for the beach resorts. During the summer of 1915, due to inclement weather recurring with marked regularity over week ends, many concessions at the beaches folded up as early as July 4.

If the sign and degree position of Saturn be carefully noted, the period of the year when maximum influences of the planet will be manifest can be timed. For example, in Pearce's Textbook of Astrology we read that "Saturn generates maximum cold in the atmosphere when occupying Aquarius." The Sun formed a conjunction with Saturn in this sign on February 8, 1934. The record low temperature of 14 degrees below zero the following day along the Atlantic Seaboard is a matter of historic record.

Saturn's conjunctions or adverse aspects with Jupiter, Uranus or Neptune are conducive to prolonged abnormal weather over certain geographic areas. These extremes of weather are frequently the motivating causes of epidemic diseases that affect a certain geographic area for a certain season and will then manifest in pandemic disease at other points quite remote in geographic longitude. Positions of the planets in relation to the solar ingress charts must be referred to in order to anticipate these areas affected. Saturn is naturally a depressant. Jupiter is related to oxygen. Saturn conjunction Jupiter affects the air through maximum carbon or dust. The air affects respiratory systems, and the blood stream is in turn affected. With reference to Saturn-Uranus configurations, we would interpret this as inclining to ranges of temperatures below the normal. Air in higher strata of atmosphere is depressed. Configurations adversely ("B") with Neptune induce excessive humidity, fogs and surface vapors that affect lowlands principally. Extreme changes.

Since, under astrological signatures, Saturn rules the bone structure, Jupiter has dominion over the blood stream, Uranus the motor nerves and Neptune the endocrine glands, the affects of weather on health conditions under the combined influence of these planets have been successfully interpreted, as we will later illustrate.

G-6—URANUS:

Uranus was discovered by Sir William Herschel, at Bath, England, on the evening of March 13, 1781. The sidereal period of this planet is 84.015 years and it remains in each sign for approximately seven years. Although affecting weather similar to Saturn's impressions, Uranus is relatively more sudden and extreme in its action for producing cold, negative electricity, increased wind velocity and atmospheric turbulence.

Effects are more potent for wind velocity in the higher altitudes and this planet appears to exert a potential influence on air currents in the very high atmospheric stratas. Uranus excites the winds from the northwest, with <u>descending</u> air currents from higher altitudes and directed downslope. Under "A" aspects, especially when forming the 60 degree angle with either Sun or Mercury, strong to fresh gales from the northwest are accompanied by appreciably lower ranges of temperature. Normally, Uranus conduces to the development of high wind pressure areas.

When occupying the 4th or 10th houses of an ingress chart or lunation map for any particular geographical point of observation, the average of temperatures for the period will range below the normal. Geographical meridians on the earth where such positions are indicated, as for example, at Tokyo, Japan, at the Winter Solstice of December 22, 1940, when Scorpio 21 culminated and Aquarius 8.32 ascended, will mark the locales of lowest temperatures, highest wind velocities and resultant damage from storms. Uranus in the lower meridian affects underground as well. This position is ever a threat either to mines or damages to property.

Winds under Uranus are <u>never</u> steady. They come straight downward, in <u>gusts</u> and spread out when they contact the surface. February winds are quite characteristic of the Uranus type. The 4th house position of Uranus at the Summer Solstice of June, 1938 traced by its lower meridian position at 71 degrees west longitude the path of the destructive hurricane which devastated Long Island and New England on September 21, 1938.

When Uranus occupies the Tropics (extreme declination), when in the equator (0°00' declination) when stationary, or when forming a conjunction, opposition or parallel of declination with the Sun, the influence of this planet for lowering the temperature and exciting wind pressure is generally manifested within three and a half days after the culmination of such positions or configurations.

Under "A" aspects which conduce to favorable weather but gusty winds and declining temperatures, it is noteworthy to mention that changes are sudden where Uranus in the key charts holds a magnetic angle to the earth. Note where Uranus occupies either the upper or lower meridian at the previous solar ingress. Then note points 90 and 45 degrees distance in geographical longitude either west or east of such meridians as focal points where maximum influences of Uranus will manifest.

The "B" and "C" inharmonious aspects of Uranus are indicative of both cold and dampness. Clouds under these configurations form like brush streaks over the western horizon, harbingers of wind and a chilly, penetrating atmosphere. In preliminary studies of this planet, note aspects formed by the Sun, Mercury, Venus or Mars. It is a remarkable fact that in winter or cold seasons, during strong Uranus aspects, (except from Venus) particularly when Mercury is configured, people may be seen running to and fro in the erratic winds. Among large cities, Chicago, in the interior, responds more frequently to the configurations of Uranus, as likewise do places in higher altitudes.

If Uranus occupy an angle at a solar ingress, observe those days when the Moon transits the upper or lower meridian at the place of observation and completes aspects with Uranus. Note also if other transiting bodies over the same points form aspects, for they will then register their effects very definitely.

G-7—NEPTUNE:

♆ The planet Neptune, which is the higher octave of the planet Venus, was discovered by Galle, of Berlin, on September 23, 1846, as the result of calculations by LeVerrier. With a diameter of over 36,500 miles and over 2,746,271,000 miles distant from the Sun, this planet completes its orbital revolution in 164.788 years. It requires an average period of approximately 13¾ years to transit through each sign.

Neptune is as spectacular in weather impressions as when otherwise applied as a principle among the heavenly arbiters. Being extreme in character, this planet accounts for many of the oddities in weather records and in seismic phenomena. Compared with the zig-zag gusts of Uranus, the planet Neptune is the celestial broom that deceives with its balmy ascending air currents, usually true vertical in the preliminary stage of its influence on the atmosphere. A soft haze with accompanying rising temperatures accompany this phenomenon and so, during its operation in cold seasons, some observers are induced by temporary flights of fancy to report premature robins or flowers poking their heads above the earth out of season.   The stagnant calm, with its accompanying hazes, is invariably a danger signal that will be followed in due course by the upper atmosphere declaring dividends of copious downfall.

The chief characteristics of Neptune are humidity, low visibility, excessive static, vacuums in higher air levels—particularly in the lowlands—prevailing southerly winds, heaviest precipitation in the lowlands that frequently lead to inundations due to fast thaws and rapidly swelling streams.   Where Neptune occupies the lower meridian in a solar ingress figure as for the meridian of St. Louis, Mo., on December 21, 1940, 4:55 p.m., such position portends downfall in excess of the seasonal average and threats of floods during the season.   A critical timing point would be when the ephemeral Sun opposes the place of Neptune or when Venus advanced to a point in quadrature to Neptune on January 11-12, 1941.

When advancing low pressure areas reach the longitude in their eastward path where Neptune occupies the meridian, they are "put through the wringer." During summer and warm seasons these disturbances are more scattered, often localized as sudden squally thunderstorms following streams of water and developing downslope.

Being very slow in motion as compared with other planets, Neptune's stations in the equator or tropics follow in turn at periods of approximately 41 years apart. Neptune will not be in the equator (0°00' declination) until November 1, 1943 and twelve days thereafter will be conjoined by Venus at that magnetic point.

Under harmonious "A" configurations, Neptune conduces to fine, warm weather, with accompanying moderate breeze and the direction of the wind varying. If configurations between cold planets also operate, then expect unsettled weather and sudden changes, particularly when higher ranges of temperature attend.

During very hot spells, any negative or "B" configurations with Neptune are most uncertain planetary influences to interpret by. It is then better to judge generally than to attempt forecasts for specific areas locally. Mars in conjunction or opposition with Neptune, and to lesser extent the quadrature aspect, should be noted carefully with reference to increasing the intensity of seismic phenomena.

Under Neptune's signature the temperature rises and humidity increases. In winter months, thaws set in, the visibility is low, smoke rises in a straight line, the atmosphere becomes saturated with aqueous vapors or fogs in the lowlands, but damp and penetrating in the interior. As winds later start precipitation downslope, the downfall is heaviest near water. In summer months Neptune's ascending air currents develop vacuums that increase intensity of the turbulence during very hot spells. Neptune storms seldom follow a straight line in one direction. 1-3-"41

1

MERCURY'S CONFIGURATIONS
IN RELATION TO WEATHER

1.01—MERCURY:

In the introductory series, the elementary principles concerning the respective planets as applicable to weather potentials were discussed. We propose now to consider effects of their various combinations with each other in geocentric longitude. Since Mercury is the swiftest moving planet and forms aspects in the heavens more rapidly than any other body except the Moon, this heavenly body is a very important factor concerning changing weather phenomena. Largely concerned with <u>wind pressure</u> and frequently with wind direction, this planet excites in the atmosphere the qualities of the planets it aspects, according to the positive (A) and negative (B and C) angles formed thereto.

1.02—MERCURY IN MAJOR STATIONS:

When in superior conjunction, in parallel of declination with, or when in greatest elongation from the Sun, this planet inclines to increased wind velocity. The same may apply when Mercury is in the equator (declination 0° 0') also when in extreme north declination and again when it attains its apparent stationary position. Geographical meridians where Mercury tenants the angles, especially the 4th or 10th mansion of the solar ingress or lunation charts, should be carefully considered as the points in longitude where such atmospheric conditions originate and move eastward. When apparently retrograde and forming conjunction or negative aspects with the Sun or major planets, Mercury is more likely to excite atmospheric turbulences that prove troublesome for means of transit and for wire communications. This planet was just turning stationary from apparent retrograde motion on September 3, 1925, when the ill-fated dirigible Shenandoah met with disaster in a wind storm. But Federal meteorologists, who then denied the influence of planets on weather, failed to recognize the significance of this phenomenon. It may be explained that these planetary positions or configurations do not exert their maximum influence over the same geographical area each time. The culmination of the aspect marks the time of influence, but Mercury's magnetic angle to specific meridians of geographical longitude must be determined from the key charts, similarly as illustrated later under statistical data.

1.03—MERCURY WITH VENUS:

When conjunction with, or in sextile or trine aspect to Venus, southerly winds are induced with accompanying elevation of temperature, gentle breezes, slight humidity and fair weather in lowlands, with light downfall in extreme north. When in opposition, square or in parallel, southerly winds veering to southeast are attended by lowering barometer, humidity, downfall along waterways from the highlands, followed by moderately lower temperatures.

1.04—MERCURY WITH MARS:

The conjunction, parallel, opposition or square configurations with Mars tend to westerly or southwest winds, dry and warmer atmosphere followed by increased wind velocity. In warm seasons thermal tendencies induce excessive static, followed by local electrical disturbances accompanied by sharp winds. In summer these combinations are potential thunderstorm breeders. In winter, fall or spring, temperatures are seasonable but wind is the chief keynote. When forming either sextile or trine aspects to Mars, Mercury induces dry, breezy weather. The effects of Mercury appear to be most potent in the lowlands when configurated with Mars, Venus, Saturn or Neptune; in highlands when aspecting Jupiter or Uranus. If Mercury should combine aspects with Mars and Saturn, or Uranus, or even Neptune near the same time, the indications for atmospheric turbulence are increased. In winter months, when Mercury and the Sun are in superior conjunction, if Mars should meanwhile form magnetic aspects, winter hurricanes and storms of sleet may be anticipated.

Winds induced by Mercury-Mars are never gentle, but rather sharp and cutting and most destructive during warm seasons.

When Mercury passes from an aspect of a warm planet like Mars to magnetic angles with a cold planet such as Saturn or Uranus while these significators are approaching an exact aspect to each other, serious atmospheric disturbances may be anticipated. When Mercury is retrograde and configured with other bodies, give preference to the negative natures of the planets concerned.

1.05—MERCURY IN ASPECTS WITH JUPITER

Under favorable "A" aspects, north to northwest winds, with rising barometer. A clear, wholesome, invigorating atmosphere. Moderate wind velocity. Temperatures remain moderate for the season. These aspects purify the atmosphere. Wool-packed fleecy clouds against a blue sky characterize these aspects. Jupiter in north declination inclines to elevate temperatures. Under negative aspects such as the opposition, square or semi-square, interpret higher wind pressure and cooler temperatures. If either planet be retrograde, expect unsettled weather. If Mars join their influence, then excessive static and, during summer or warm seasons, expect electrical phenomena.

1.06—MERCURY IN ASPECTS WITH SATURN:

In positive "A" aspects with Saturn, indicates upslope winds from the lowlands, partly cloudy, moderately humid and cooler, building up low pressure areas in the interior and highlands. Inclines to southeast winds. Barometer is moderately lower in lowlands with increasing depression in the interior. All aspects between Mercury and Saturn are potential cloud breeders. Under negative "B" aspects, particularly the conjunction, opposition or square with Saturn, gradually increasing cloudiness, easterly winds, lowering barometer and condensation of moisture. Temperature declines gradually during warm months along waterways. In cold seasons fogs, thaws and downfall in the lowlands, often followed by the long northeasters along the coast and cold waves in the interior. Saturn weather develops slowly, though is effective and enduring. These Mercury-Saturn storms produce penetrating cold waves on their northern and western tangents. Easterly winds and a mephitic atmosphere [noxious–editor] precede the approaching center of these storms. Dull, damp atmosphere is the chief characteristic of conflicting Mercury-Saturn aspects, especially the conjunction.

1.07—MERCURY IN ASPECTS WITH URANUS:

When in favorable ("A") trine, sextile or semi-sextile aspects, fair and colder, with descending air currents. Gusty. Mercury and Uranus invariably excite winds. Temperatures decline quickly. Cold waves, in the highlands of the interior, sweep down from the northwest. Winds also come down straight from aloft and spread out at the surface. Sextile aspect is most potent in this respect.

Under negative "B" configurations, including the parallel, similar winds accompanied by bleak skies. Air very penetrating. Conjunction and opposition between these bodies are both hurricane breeders. In winter months, when attendant phenomena accentuate low pressure areas, these combinations play havoc with telephone and telegraph lines due to snow, sleet and high velocity winds. This planetary combination imparts maximum negative electricity in the atmosphere, hence conducing to cold and wind in gusts. The impressions of Uranus are always spasmodic and zig-zag. Owing to the downward sweep of cold air, with barometer abnormally high, low pressure areas of similar intensity will often precede or follow the "high." Between the two areas is a danger zone for aviation.

In early spring, late summer or early fall, these configurations, particularly the conjunction or opposition, are harbingers of hurricanes in the Caribbean Sea and warmer climates to the South.

Mercury on the lower meridian at an ingress or lunation and combining its influence with Uranus, predicates serious damage to property as the results of storms and high wind velocity. If this happens in the 3rd house, then such atmospheric conditions have their origin to the westward of the observation point. If in the 10th house, the high pressure areas are veering southward of the observation point, or following southerly course from west to east.

1.08—MERCURY IN ASPECTS WITH NEPTUNE:
Mercury's configurations with Neptune operate in a manner similar to influences on weather when forming angles with the planet Venus, but the effects are more extreme. The positive "A" aspects are conducive to southerly winds, rising temperatures, moderate humidity, gentle breezes. Wind direction is inclined to shift in the highlands, but the weather is generally fair.

The negative "B" and "C" aspects including the conjunction and parallel, indicate variable winds, ranging generally upslope from lowlands to highlands. In warm seasons, if humidity ranges high in lowlands and valleys and southerly winds prevail, barometric depression develops to the northward. Local storms then working southward, against the wind, follow along waterways. Weather is unsettled. In winter and cold seasons, humid and cloudy, often indicating smoke fogs over low cities. Shifting winds, with freakish atmospheric conditions. During very hot summer weather these aspects indicate lowering barometer, stagnant atmosphere, sudden changes. If heat producing phenomena attend, sudden squalls of local character may be expected. Air currents are for most part vertical ascending and static conditions are increased. The conjunction is usually attended by local squalls in summer.

1:09—STATISTICAL DATA - MERCURY:

(a) On July 24, 1926, Mercury, <u>stationary</u> in Leo 21.13, in partile <u>conjunction with Neptune</u> and <u>square a stationary Saturn</u> in Scorpio 19.25. A gale attaining a velocity of 105 miles an hour unroofed buildings at Seagirt, Manasquan and other New Jersey coast towns. The storm hit from the west and damage to property along the New Jersey coast was estimated at $100,000. (Refer to 1.02).

(b) Continuing retrograde, Mercury formed a <u>conjunction with the Sun</u> on August 7, 1926. A hurricane originating in the Caribbean Sea coursed northward over the Bermudas and along the Atlantic Seaboard to the Banks of Newfoundland where it played havoc with maritime shipping. The German liner Deutschland , bound for New York City, reported having encountered a 100 mile-an-hour gale, together with mountainous high seas. (1.02, 1.06, 1.08).

(c) Mercury, retrograde, was in <u>conjunction with the Sun</u> on April 19, 1925. Fourteen inches of snowfall was reported at Woodside, N. H. The <u>superior conjunction</u> of Mercury with the <u>Sun</u> on October 7, 1925 was preceded on the 6th by an earthquake in Helena, Montana. A cold wave followed a snowstorm eastward. On October 7, winds of high velocity struck Chicago and the temperature dropped 20 degrees overnight. (0.04).

(d) Mercury <u>stationary</u> in Sagittarius 11.20R November 15, 1926. Strong gales troubled shipping along Atlantic Seaboard. Again, on November 25, 1926, Mercury in Sagittarius, retrograde and <u>conjunction with the Sun</u>, a tornado from central Arkansas cut northward through Missouri. 84 persons killed and more than 300 injured. Property damage estimated above a million dollars. Heavy rains in New York City on evening of 26th, with barometer 29.64 at 10 p.m. N. W. gales and cold wave followed on November 27, the temperature declining to 28 at 7:30 p.m. (0.04)

(e) November 28, 1926. Mercury retrograde and <u>conjunction with Saturn</u>. A cold wave hit New York City on December 1. Temperature dropped to 12 degrees at 5.00 am, on December 3, accompanied by first snow of season as <u>Mercury trined Uranus</u>. (1.06) (1.07).

(f) A striking instance of the influence of <u>Mercury when in an angle</u> at the seasonal ingresses was indicated at the Winter Solstice for Washington, D.C., December 21, 1887, 9:56 p.m. Mercury occupied the 4th angle or lower meridian and formed a sextile aspect to Uranus. From these testimonies the historical blizzard of March 8, 1888 was predicted by A.J. Pearce a year in advance, in Zadkiel's Almanac. (1.02)

(g) Galveston Flood, Sept 8, 1900, Mercury, in Virgo 8° 38', had formed an exact quadrature aspect to Uranus, in Sagittarius, on Sept. 7.   Three days previous, Saturn had attained a stationary position in Sagittarius 28° 26' where it opposed Neptune in Gemini 29° 02', a combination conducive to building up excessive humidity and abnormal weather conditions. On September 8, at 3:41 p.m., the Moon, in Pisces 8° 38', opposed Mercury and squared Uranus at Galveston. Between 6:20 and 8:30 p.m. the wind attained a velocity of 120 miles per hour when the anemometer was blown away. Water rose four feet in a few minutes at 7:30 p.m. In this disaster, 6,000 lives were lost. Months in advance, Rev. Irl Hicks, editor of Hicks' Weather Almanac, had printed and circulated at his own expense, advance warnings of a disastrous storm to be expected in that area, even plotting its time and general course, but he was ridiculed by official forecasters for his efforts.

(h) Mercury conjunction Uranus on lower meridian. At the solar eclipse on March 7, 1932, 2:46 a.m., E.S.T., Aries 18 was on the lower meridian and Uranus tenanted this position at Long. 86° W. Mercury formed a conjunction with Uranus on the lower meridian at this meridian on March 21, in Aries 18.15. On that date a violent tornado wrought destruction to property and incurred mortalities in Alabama at Long. 87 W. and Lat. 33 N., then swept through South Carolina and parts of Tennessee, Georgia and Kentucky. 200 persons were reported dead and approximately 1,000 injured in this devastating storm.   (1.07)

(i) Mercury opposition Uranus: On September 19, 1926, Mercury formed a conjunction with the Sun and both bodies forming an opposition to Uranus, thus accentuating high wind pressure, high barometer and descending air currents. A hurricane devastated Miami, Fla on Sept. 17-18, then veered to Mobile and Pensacola. (0.04 -1.02 -1.07)

(j) Again, on September 10, 1928, while Mercury and Uranus were forming an opposition, a terrific hurricane developed several hundred miles east of Puerto Rico and swept across that island, incurring loss of life and enormous damage to property. The storm entered Florida on Sept. 16 at 6:00 p.m. incurring millions of dollars loss in property damage and causing deaths of 1500 persons. As a high pressure area blanketed the storm from the west wing, the hurricane followed a course northward to Cape Hatteras. U.P. dispatches from Flomaton, Fla. [AL–*editor*] reported that the wind velocity had reached a maximum of ninety-five miles an hour. Since that time, Florida has increased safeguards for better protection against such storms.

(k) <u>Mercury conjunction Sun</u>. On November 11, 1940, Mercury's transit over the Sun's disk—a perfect conjunction—again verified Mercury's reputation for exciting high wind velocity and blizzards in winter under this configuration (0.04). Storm potentials had been building up in geographical areas considerably to the westward since Mercury opposed Uranus on November 7 (1.07). On November 11, when the actual transit across the Sun took place, tornadoes, blizzards and gales wrought havoc in twenty western and southern States. Storms carried the first major cold wave of the season, with a temperature of 21 degrees below zero reported in Montana. Wind velocity at Detroit's airport was measured at 78 miles per hour. The worst storm on Lake Michigan in twenty years and the hardest blow in Chicago since 1898 were reported. Property damage amounting to millions of dollars was reported in Chicago, Detroit and St. Louis. In New York, where Mars and Neptune had occupied the lower meridian at the autumnal ingress, comparatively milder weather accompanied the storm's eastward path. In New York City, overcast skies and rain continued from November 11 to 15 inclusive. (1.02)

Our records indicate that a similar transit of Mercury over the Sun's disk occurred on May 7, 1924, the Sun setting with Mercury on the disk only partly visible at Washington, 4:44 p.m. A check up of weather records over western States for that date and into May 8 should reveal high wind velocities.

(l) <u>Mercury Stationary</u>: August 12, 1925. Winds of high velocity in New York. On December 1, 1925, Mercury and Uranus both stationary. Hurricane in Miami, Fla. (0.03)

2

VENUS'S CONFIGURATIONS IN RELATION TO WEATHER

2.01—GENERAL:

VENUS symbolizes the copper element in nature's batteries. Winds, under the action of this planet on weather, are gentle and principally from a southerly direction. In primary stations, i.e., occupying the North Tropic, crossing the Equator, or when attaining a stationary position, this planet conduces to increased humidity, lowering barometer, gentle winds, misty to foggy weather, increasing cloudiness and downfall. In ingress or lunation maps, Venus occupying the meridian is indicative of downfall in excess or the normal for the period. If a winter quarter be concerned, this indicates heavy snowfalls, usually preceded by balmy spells over the southern areas. In warmer seasons, sultry and warm, followed by heavy showers. Venus in the North Tropic during summer months usually is accompanied by prolonged spells of hot, sticky weather that cause so much discomfiture in the lowlands. This planet is productive of more downfall in Taurus or Scorpio, Cancer or Pisces, of fogs when tenanting Capricorn and cold, freezing rain or snow when in Aquarius. In Aquarius, downfalls are cold drizzles followed by cold waves. The two inferior planets also change their impressions according to configurations with the respective major planets. In the following interpretations note especially the considerable variations of influences on either moisture or temperature between aspects to Mars, Saturn, Uranus and Neptune respectively.

2.02 - VENUS WITH THE SUN:

Venus in sextile aspect with the Sun is strongest for fair, mild weather, while other harmonious (A) aspects operate similarly and in less degree for higher range of temperatures. The conjunction with the Sun, particularly when Venus is retrograde, indicates rising temperature with accompanying humidity, lowering barometer, increasing cloudiness, preponderating south winds and heavy downfall. Likewise interpret for the parallel of declination, or opposition, the 90 degree and 45 degree angles, with strength of influence ranging in the order given. Venus configurations from the sign Scorpio incline to dark low clouds with "sloppy" weather. Downfall is heavier when Venus occupies watery signs under the aspects or near the same time occupies major stations. In cold signs (extreme southern declination) prolonged overcast weather, fogs or slow cold drizzles are characterized. High wind velocities are usually absent under the influence of Venus, but cooler temperatures usually follow downfalls under this planet even during the hottest seasons.

2.03—VENUS WITH MARS:

The positive configurations between Venus and Mars, particularly the sextile or trine angles, incline to higher ranges of temperature and fair weather. But since the general tendency of Venus is to make moisture pregnant, it is necessary to allow for flexibility in applying any rules combining Venus and Mars configurations. In any aspect they are productive of rising temperature. It is difficult to set up any hard and fast rules relative to showers under the harmonious (A) aspects, since judgment must necessarily be guided by the relative strength of either significator, by north declination, equatorial or sign position as well as probable angular position westward of the point of observation in order to determine whether the thermal principle of Mars or the humid, moist principle of Venus will predominate.

When Venus forms a conjunction with Mars, the moist nature of the former is energized and, following a sharp rise in temperature, showery weather may be expected. The chief characteristic is dashing rain, accompanied by very moderate wind velocity. If Venus be retrograde, showers may materialize under any aspects as local showers during warm seasons, in the lowlands. Note whether the Moon occupies the Equator, the North Tropic, or if it is in perigee at the time such configurations culminate, for such positions tend to increase the downfall. Influences of both planets are most potent in the lowlands, along the coast and in atmospheric stratas nearest the surface of the earth. If Venus be near the South Tropic or occupying the sign of Aquarius, colder rain accompanied by prolonged drizzles and followed by much colder temperatures may be anticipated. It should be borne in mind that showers under the configurations of these planets will usually culminate closer to the time of aspects during hot seasons, but after the aspect has formed during the winter and cooler seasons. If the Moon forms a conjunction or square with either significator a day or two before the actual completion of their aspects, their combined qualities will then be generated ahead of time. In all aspects between planets, give due consideration to the Moon as a contributory time marker in the same respect that we observe the Sun as a potential time marker in weather potentials.

2.04—VENUS WITH JUPITER:

The conjunction, parallel of declination, sextile or trine angles between Venus and Jupiter are conducive to fresh, serene and temperate atmosphere that favors out-of-door activities. Regardless of existing weather conditions, these combinations tend to clear the atmosphere. Temperatures are moderate, but incline to higher ranges if the Sun meanwhile aspects one of the arbiters. If Mars combines with these configurations, excessive temperatures, especially in warm seasons, may induce atmospheric disturbances.

Venus forming opposition, square or semi-square angles to Jupiter will generally incline to gentle south winds at the surface and north winds aloft, inducing cloudy weather. Brief local showers in summer months.

2.05—VENUS WITH SATURN:

Since the chief characteristics of Saturn, weatherwise, are dullness, depression and shadows under the adverse configurations and concentration of cold under the harmonious angles as compared with the acute, energetic and sharp penetrating impressions of the calorific Mars, it follows that the configurations with Saturn are slower and more enduring in developing weather changes. The crystallizing influences of Saturn under the 60 degree angle formed by Venus, or when Saturn at the time occupies a primary station, invariably indicate lower ranges of temperature. Where downfall happens under any Venus-Saturn combinations, lowering temperatures gradually follow, the coldness being more intense in the interior.

Venus and Saturn in sextile, trine or weaker semi-sextile aspects are conducive to cooler but fair weather, even though broken clouds may moderate the sunshine. The sextile, or 60 degree, angle indicates high barometric pressure, moderate wind velocity and lower temperature. During cold seasons, expect cold waves and frosts.

The conjunction, opposition, square or semi-square of Venus with Saturn are indicative of lowering barometer, easterly winds, gradually increasing cloudiness with characteristic dull, leaden skies. The atmosphere becomes decidedly damp and chilly, due to excessive humidity. Heaviest downfall attends these phenomena, under predominating easterly winds. Prolonged northeasters may continue for many hours. Downfall if these aspects are preceded by south winds and warm temperatures. In winter, rain turning to sleet or snow, especially it Venus be in south declination. In spring or autumn seasons, fogs frequently develop along the coast and lowlands. In warm seasons heavy, prolonged rains.

If other configurations indicating cold temperatures attend these phenomena, then expect slow, cold rain—sometimes cold, intermittent drizzle. Low hanging, dark clouds generally accompany or follow these aspects. Inside amusements thrive during such periods of foul weather. In judging effects of the parallel, downfall will be heavy if both bodies are near conjunction or opposition.

The sleepy, dull feeling so frequently experienced by individuals during so-called "rotten" weather under these configurations is not attributable so much to the weather as to human reaction to the configurations directly. Note affects of these planetary combinations on peach crops during growing seasons.

2.06—VENUS WITH URANUS:

The positive sextile, trine, semi-sextile and most particularly the sextile (60 degree) angle of Venus to Uranus indicate high barometer and <u>brilliant</u> atmosphere even though the temperature declines appreciably. Wind velocity is moderate. These aspects are generally conducive to fine weather for outdoor photography, sky-writing or other activities where clear visibility and unlimited ceiling are salient features. Very cold aloft. In early fall or late spring, sudden frosts may be expected. Temperatures decline sharply at night. Effects of these combined significators are likely to develop very rapidly. Downfall frequently occurs <u>prior</u> to the culmination of these aspects.

Negative: When Venus forms a conjunction or parallel with Uranus, especially if either body be in apparent retrograde motion, there is likely to be cold, drizzling rain. Spasmodic winds contribute to a raw, penetrating, cold atmosphere. The opposition, square and semi-square aspects likewise indicate low, dark clouds, wind and slow rain, accompanied by low ranges of temperature. The wind eventually veers to the northwest and temperatures fall rapidly, with cold waves developing in the interior. If Mercury adds its influence during late autumn, in winter, or early spring, sleet and snow storms impede traffic and communication lines. Venus forming aspects from Aquarius brings more cold.

Observations over a period of more than thirty years seem to indicate that atmospheric static reaches a minimum under combined action of Venus and Uranus and that barometric pressure is abnormally high, particularly when they form an angle of 60 degrees. These aspects, therefore, seem to be most favorable for important radio transmission and reception between remote distant points.

2.07—<u>VENUS WITH NEPTUNE</u>:

Under any angles between Venus and Neptune, southerly winds preponderate, the temperature rises, the air is misty, the barometer falls gradually. Humidity is a chief characteristics, wind velocity is at minimum. Under the favorable trine, sextile and 30 degree semi-sextile angles, expect calm, misty atmosphere accompanied by higher ranges of temperature. Very sultry in warmer seasons. Humid in lowlands especially. During summer cloudy in highlands, with local showers.

Venus forming conjunction or parallel of declination with Neptune charges the atmosphere with a maximum of humidity. No wind velocity apparent. Smoke rises vertically. Air is warm but sultry and in warm months oppressive. Cloudiness builds up rapidly. The square, opposition and semi-square similarly impress the atmosphere. Heaviest downpours occur under these configurations. Precipitation is torrential within a short period of time. The conjunction of these bodies on the lower meridian is a threat of floods, usually operating within narrow or limited areas.

These harbingers of inundations, when operating jointly, are more effective in the lowlands along the coast and waterways. One of the peculiar characteristics of the rainfall developing under the conjunction is that its develops rather suddenly, frequently unexpected by the official weather forecasters, and is restricted to localized areas in lowlands, starting in northern areas and progressing southward against the approaching upslope winds. Note where either Venus or Neptune occupies the lower meridian at the preceding solar ingress, for at such meridians, the downfall for the season should be greatest. For illustration: At the Autumnal Equinox on September 23, 1937, 11:23 am, London, Virgo 19 occupied the upper meridian at London and thru that meridian north and south. Neptune was exactly on the meridian, in Virgo 19.08. When Venus formed a conjunction with this degree on October 11, 1937, torrential rains were reported from Spain and other parts of Southern Europe, since the configuration fell in the <u>south</u> angle of the map.

It is only by means of applying these principles to the key charts transposed for various meridians in longitude that one may determine whether the various types of atmospheric phenomena may veer southward or northward over given geographical points on the earth.

2.08—Venus: Statistical Data:

(a) The chart below for the Winter Solstice on December 22, 1917, 75th meridian, was used by us in 1917 as a basis for forecasting not only a severe winter season to follow, but also extremely low temperatures for the closing days of December and during the second week of February. At first examination, the position of Mars, (southing) might lead the interpreter to deduce that a higher range of temperatures would be indicated over the Atlantic Seaboard. Nevertheless, the rule regarding the efficacy of planets in angles is subject to qualifications when two or more planets occupy strong positions in the 3rd and 9th houses or when forming important configurations therefrom.

Uranus tenanting the nadir at 86 degrees west longitude and occupying Aquarius, the coldest of all signs, was the primary basis

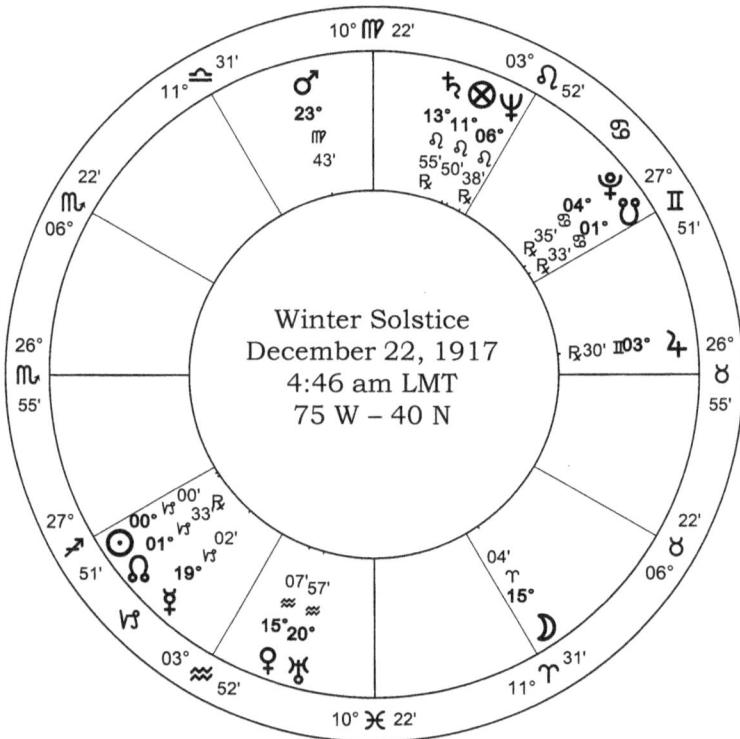

Winter Solstice
December 22, 1917
4:46 am LMT
75 W – 40 N

of our interpretation. Venus, also in Aquarius, was applying to a conjunction with Uranus. Mercury, the blizzard breeder, was moving up to those focal points. On December 30, 1917, when Venus transited the radical place of Uranus in the figure, the temperature at New York City registered 13° below zero: Venus, after attaining a stationary position in Aquarius 28.29 on January 21, 1918, retrograded back to a conjunction with Uranus on February 9 and the cold wave was repeated. Note Saturn, in the opposite point, applying to an opposition with Uranus.

From the foregoing it will be seen that strength of planets in "cold" or "hot" signs are equally as important as configurations when venturing weather prognoses. (refer 2.06)

(b) VENUS CONJUNCTION MARS, August 30, 1927. On August 28 preceding, the Moon formed a conjunction with both planets thereby exciting the influence of the conjunction before the time of its actual culmination. On that date 4.18 inches of rain fell at Albany, N.Y. within 24 hours (2.03).

(c) VENUS IN THE EQUATOR, August 7, 1927. On August 8, a torrential downpour developed in New York City, a downfall of 2.79 inches being recorded. Again, on April 14, 1928, when Venus was in the equator, Chile, South America was snowed under with a twelve foot downfall. (Their autumn season down there.) At New York, on the same date, southerly winds preceded showery weather. Thirteen inches of snow fell in southern Minnesota. Heavy snow and sleet fell at Dallas, Texas. Blizzards, with accompanying drops of 25 degrees in temperature, were reported sweeping eastward in many Central States as Mercury conjunction Uranus in Aries 4.32 attended this equatorial station of Venus. (G-2 and 1.07).

(d) In the chart for the full Moon on November 9, 1927, 1:36 a.m., 75th meridian, Gemini 13 occupied the Midheaven and Virgo 15.23 ascended. Saturn tenanted the lower meridian at 81 degrees west longitude. The Sun and Mercury were conjoined in the 3rd house of the figure. Mercury was retrograde and its actual transit over the Sun's disc happened on the lower meridian at 103 degrees west during the late evening of the 9th. On the same date, Venus was forming an exact opposition to Uranus, with both planets in the equatorial degrees. A low pressure area drifted eastward, preceded by warm southerly winds. Venus was in the equator on November 10. A cold wave developed over Minnesota, Iowa, Nebraska, Kansas and Colorado, temperatures dropping 20 degrees rather suddenly. Winter whistled into Chicago on the 11th at 5:00 p.m. on the wings of a 90 mile an hour gale, almost a tornado in spots. A boy was killed by lightning at Milwaukee (in November!). In Chicago, 12 persons were injured and enormous property damage was reported in the storm area. At Chicago, the temperature dropped 28 degrees in three hours. (Compare with 1.09k, Mercury transiting Sun's disc. 2.08d).

(e) DISASTROUS FLOODS IN MISSISSIPPI VALLEY, January 1-25, 1937:

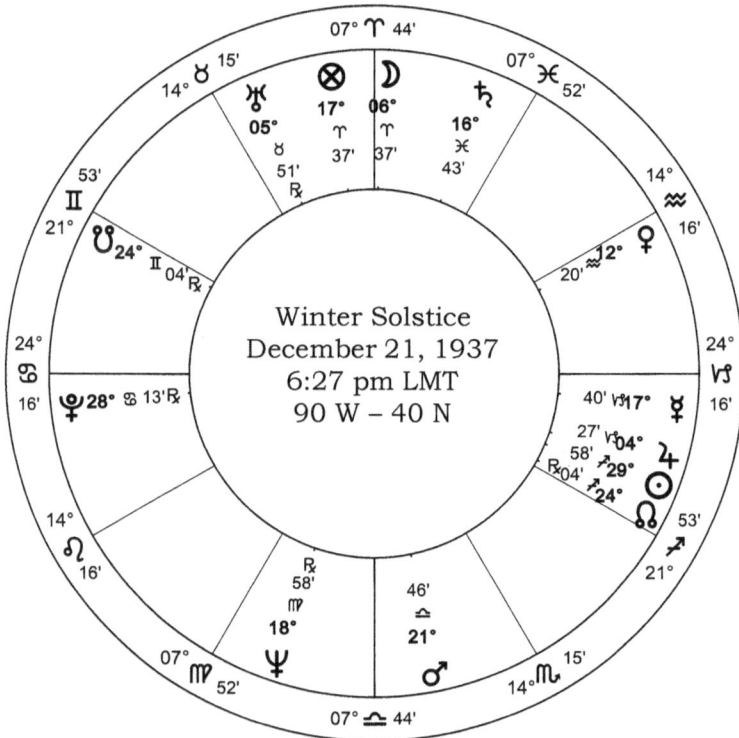

Winter Solstice
December 21, 1937
6:27 pm LMT
90 W – 40 N

The approaching important opposition between the two major planets Saturn and Neptune (excessive humidity and barometric depression indicators), that became exact on January 18, 1937, was primarily responsible for the excessive precipitation in the Mississippi Valley during that period. At the preceding Winter Solstice, the Moon was exactly culminating at the 90th meridian. The Saturn opposition Neptune accumulated moisture from points westward. At the 75th meridian, Mars was situated on the lower meridian where Aries 21 occupied the Midheaven and Leo 3.37 ascended. This position predicated a comparatively warmer and dryer season for the eastern sections of the country. Neptune fell on the nadir at 105 degrees west longitude. The point of saturation developed midway between these meridians, which was at Cairo, Illinois.

The effects of the static Saturn opposition Neptune were intensified on January 21 by Venus parallel Neptune on January 21, on January 22 by its opposition to Neptune and on January 23 by its conjunction with Saturn. On January 24, the Sun formed a semi-square with Saturn. According to records of the U. S. Weather Bureau, a total of 20 inches of rain fell between January 1 and 25th in the territory just south of Cairo, Illinois, where the Ohio and Mississippi Rivers joined. (Refer to 2.05, 2.07 and G-7, page 19.)

(f) VENUS ON THE MERIDIAN AT SOLAR INGRESS:
    In the map for the Winter Solstice, on December 22, 1930, 8:40 a.m. 75th Meridian, Scorpio 12.00 occupied the Midheaven and Venus tenanted the south angle, in Scorpio 23.42. During the winter season covered by that chart, we observed that low pressure areas from the west veered southward as they approached the Atlantic Seaboard. On January 7, however, under Sun conjunction Mercury and Saturn and opposition Jupiter, while one of the severest blizzards in years was blanketing upper New York State with two feet of snow, sharp earthquake tremors, at 7:15 p.m., at Ottawa and points in Quebec, Canada, were reported to be the sharpest since 1925.

(g) Dr. Goad, in his Astro-Meteorologica, founded on observations of thirty years, avers that Venus or Mercury with the planet Jupiter, in the seismic sign Taurus, are conducive to earth tremors.

(h) VENUS IN THE NORTH TROPIC:
    An interesting map for studying the influence of Venus in the Tropic of Cancer and also occupying the upper meridian of a Summer Solstice map is that for the Summer Solstice for St. Louis, Mo. on June 21, 1941 where Cancer 13 occupies the Midheaven and Libra 8.20 the ascendant. Venus, tenanting the south angle, in Cancer 16.55, is conjoined by Mercury R. in 15.31. Such a combination is indicative of excessive humidity and sultry atmosphere, with low pressure areas drifting southward and precipitation for the season being above the normal. In Astrotech, November 1, 1940, where a copy of the ingress map was presented, we ventured these observations in advance. Venus in the North Tropic is usually indicative of warm, humid and sultry atmosphere for days. Then follows a period of showery weather, whereby the humidity that has

been building up, is dissipated.

With respect to this ingress map for various meridians, it is interesting to note that the cold, crystallizing sign Aquarius occupies the lower meridian (the earth's magnetic angle) or polar opposite, at the 80th meridian and Eastward.   This is the area where condensation of the humid atmosphere drifting from the west may be expected.   3-7-41.

3

MARS'S CONFIGURATIONS
IN RELATION TO WEATHER

3.01—<u>GENERAL</u>

MARS symbolizes the red ray in the solar spectrum, reflects positive electricity and its general nature inclines to evaporation, preponderantly westerly winds, with rising temperatures. Action of this planet is rapid and it might very aptly be referred to as the celestial spark plug which ignites or energizes nature's batteries. The most intense droughts, heat waves, static conditions and fire hazards resulting from spontaneous combustion have been observed to accompany the positions of this calorific planet in its major stations.

Of chief consideration among these major stations is when Mars is in <u>perigee</u> at periods of approximately 1.88 years (when it is then closest to the earth). Positive electricity in the atmosphere with attendant higher ranges of temperature and prevailing dryness are observed in proportion to the nearness of Mars to the earth, the closest being 34,000,000 miles. Forest fires and inflammatory ailments also accompany this phenomenon. Insurance companies might benefit by seeking the relation between epidemics of smallpox, scarlatina and like feverish ailments with the cycles of Mars. The geographical meridian where Mars happens to be on the lower meridian of the solar ingress just prior to the time of perigee should be computed as the point where maximum effects may be expected to manifest, secondly, the upper meridian or where ascending or setting.

When Mars is in <u>perihelion</u> (closest to the Sun) a higher range of temperatures than the average for the season may be expected. When a planet is on the lower meridian at a solar ingress, the greatest intensity of the electromagnetic currents are focussed through the earth at that particular longitude. Observe those days when the Sun forms aspects to the position of Mars or when the Moon forms a conjunction, opposition or square to the position in the key chart.

These points should be considered with reference to positions on the meridian in all cases. In July, 1926, the perihelion station of Mars was accompanied by waves of heat over the Eastern States and temperatures of 102 degrees were recorded. The perihelion on October 30, 1937 was also followed by higher average ranges of temperature and dry weather. Mars was then conjunction Jupiter near the South Tropic and greatest intensity of heat was thus concentrated in the Southern Hemisphere.

Mars in the equator, occupying the North Tropic (extreme north declination), as in June, 1938, or when tenanted on the lower meridian of a solar ingress, as on December 21, 1936, 7:18 p.m., L.M.T., Washington, D.C., conduces to higher seasonal temperatures and dryness above the normal average. Calcination or generation of heat is strongest when Mars occupies the sign Leo during warm seasons. If the Sun and Mars should form a conjunction in Leo, their combined influence generates burning heat. The key notes of Mars are energy, penetration and speed.

When Mars combines its rays with Saturn, Uranus, Neptune or Mercury, atmospheric turbulences are generated. Combined with Jupiter, heat and thunder. When stationary, the temperature rises.

3.03—MARS WITH THE SUN:
When Mars is configured with the Sun the temperature rises. The conjunction and 60 degree aspects are strongest in this respect, then the trine and 30 degree angles, in relative strength of influence as in the order given. The parallel of declination, when both are north or south in declination, operates similar to the conjunction and frequently more effectively. If one significator has opposite declination to the other, then storms with destructive winds may follow. In warmer seasons, the more intense the heat waves attending these phenomena, the greater the atmospheric disturbances to follow. The conjunction and opposition of Mars with the Sun appear to have disturbing effects on ocean currents. When Mars is in south declination, currents in the southern hemisphere are affected; when in north declination, ocean currents in the northern hemisphere are disturbed under such configurations. Under the negative opposition, square, semi-square or 135 degree aspects between the Sun and Mars, it is advisable to consider the Sun's sign position for seasonal character. In warm seasons particularly, these configurations, by strength in the order given, stir up atmospheric disturbances over restricted areas, with intensity in proportion to the high temperatures generated. In cooler seasons sharp winds

from the west.

3.04—MARS WITH JUPITER:
Planets with faster motion apply by aspect to planets with slower motion. This is the order in which we present various planetary configurations for reference.

The <u>conjunction</u> of Mars and Jupiter, particularly when both planets have north declination or occupy the meridian of an ingress chart, is one of the strongest combinations for extremes of high temperatures for the season, followed by intense electrical phenomena. Under this combination in northern signs, thunderstorms manifest <u>even in mid-winter</u>. In summer or warm seasons, electrical reactions follow in proportion to the intensity of the heat wave. In all seasons, any aspects between these two bodies induce a rising mercury. The 60 degree angle is conducive to heat and drought, but electrical reactions are less likely, unless Saturn, Uranus or Neptune combine their configurations.

All negative aspects between Mars and Jupiter, including the opposition, square and 45 degree angle, also the parallel of declination, are sudden storm breeders as soon as a northwest wind sets in. One must necessarily observe whether cold planets like Uranus or Saturn combine their influences, as conflicting currents then disturb the atmosphere. Jupiter represents oxygen and therefore, when Mars combines its fiery ray, we may logically account for the increased number of fires, including forest fires as may be indicated on April 2, 1942 when they form a conjunction in Gemini 15. These conjunctions develop evaporation rapidly and near the time of such phenomena observations have indicated an increase in the number of fires resulting from spontaneous combustion. Sometimes, in winter, during the coldest weather, sharp winds, following temporary "warm" spells under Mars-Jupiter configurations are also provocative of increased fire hazards.

3.05—MARS WITH SATURN:
Since Mars inclines to warmth, reflects positive electricity and symbolizes the <u>red</u> ray in the solar spectrum while Saturn, reflecting negative electricity, the blue ray of light and inducing humidity inclines to barometric depression, these planets are diametrically opposite to each other in character. Saturn condenses or crystallizes aqueous vapors. The influence of Mars promotes evaporation. The result is conflicting currents in the atmosphere, promoting varying winds and destructive storms in the lowlands when these major

planets form their conjunction, parallel of declination, opposition or square aspects to each other. The atmospheric disturbances are most intense when these configurations, particularly the conjunction, take place during the warm seasons.

The sextile, trine, semi-sextile and 150 degree angles incline to cloudy weather with wind. Indeed, all configurations between Mars and Saturn, especially in cold seasons, promote wind. When these planets are combined in aspects, their influence is akin to that of Uranus.

A. J. Pearce, in his "Science of the Stars" observes that the conjunction of Mars and Saturn in the zodiacal sign Cancer, which happens once in 30 years, is of major importance. Such a conjunction took place on September 10, 1915, 11:38 p.m., E.S.T., in Cancer 14.25. Records of our personal observations at that time indicate that violent storms in New York at that time caused considerable damage to property. On September 11, at 6:55 p.m. when a building was struck by lightning a four alarm fire resulted in $1,000,000 property loss. Due to flood conditions, short circuits developed in the New York subway system on three different dates. Following unusually stormy weather in the southern States, floods developed in Louisiana. Preceding the storm at New York on September 11, when the Moon squared both Mars and Saturn, the temperature rose to 100 degrees. The next conjunction of Mars and Saturn in Cancer 24.48 on October 26, 1945 is recommended to astronomers for research.

3.06—MARS WITH URANUS:

Effects from this planetary combination are usually acute in culminating and receding. Under any aspects whatsoever, Mars and Uranus are provocative of wind velocity. Under the sextile, trine, semi-sextile and 150 degree angles between these heavenly bodies, the general tendency is variable winds of increasing velocity accompanied by broken clouds. Atmospheric conditions are usually referred to as "breezy" and wind direction veers from west to northwest.

The negative opposition, square, semi-square and 135 degree configurations, including the conjunction of these major planets, are similar in character to the influences of like configurations between Mars and Saturn, yet comparatively more rapid. The conjunction and opposition are particularly violent weatherwise, especially during the warm seasons. All negative configurations are unfavorable to aviation in the upper air levels, due to erratic wind currents ascending and descending as high and low pressure areas are formed adjacent to each other. In warmer seasons these powerful and violent combinations of Mars and Uranus are conducive to "line squalls" coming out of the west. Both of these planetary bodies are strongly electrical in character, being positive and negative respectively. When such aspects are preceded by high ranges of temperature, atmospheric reactions are characterized by low and moisture-laden black clouds attended by electrical phenomena and often resulting in devastating storms along very narrow paths. These storms invariably catch the federal weather forecasters unawares, insofar as 24 hour weather forecasts are concerned. Note particularly those geographic meridians where either Mars or Uranus occupy the north or south angle in the solstice or lunar-quarter maps.

In this respect, the chart for the Full Moon on May 11, 1941, 0:16 a.m. Eastern Standard Time, provides interesting study. Scorpio 25 occupies the midheaven, Aquarius 2.28 ascends. Uranus, in 25.49 Taurus, is exactly on the lower meridian at New York City. Five other heavenly bodies, including the Sun, are all bunched near the lower meridian and also in the sign Taurus—a very rare phenomenon. Mars, in the ascendant, is just separating from the square of Uranus, Mercury squares Mars and conjoins Uranus. But of chief significance on May 11, is the Moon on the upper meridian opposing all the six bodies on the lower meridian and squaring Mars, thus bringing to perfection the combined cross currents of all those electromagnetic forces, which also produce the sunspots, the odd electrical and magnetic storms and even 90 mile-an-hour gales attending the conjunction of Jupiter and Uranus on and after May 8. In the face of these advance forecasts and observed effects six weeks later which should confirm them, lay minds can judge for themselves the relation between the planetary phenomena and the terrestrial reactions.

3.07—MARS WITH NEPTUNE:
All configurations of Mars and Neptune impress the atmosphere similarly as aspects between Venus and Mars, since Neptune is the higher octave of the planet Venus. The Mars-Neptune configurations, however, are more extreme and productive of freak changes.

The sextile, trine, 30 degree and 150 degree aspects are conducive to rising temperature, ascending air currents and a sultry atmosphere, especially in the lowlands. Static conditions increase under all configurations between these bodies.

Under <u>negative</u> aspects, which include the conjunction, opposition, square of 90 degrees and angles of 45 and 135 degrees, rated in strength of influence in the order mentioned, static electricity is intensified in the atmosphere, particularly during periods of prevailing high temperatures. Temperatures rise, peculiar calms ensue and are followed by squally storms of short duration over narrow areas in the lowlands. Barometric pressure falls rapidly. These atmospheric disturbances are more intense during the summer, late spring and early fall months. Near water, the air is sultry and a yellowish haze accompanies the rising temperature. In warm seasons <u>local</u> thunderstorms preceded by squally winds from the west, cut narrow paths over lowlands, particularly along the coast and are menacing to aviation and small sailing craft. These aspects operate very close to the time of their culmination if the Sun or Moon happen to form angles to both bodies near the time of aspect.   3-28-41

3.08—THE PLANET MARS IN RELATION TO WEATHER-STATISTICAL DATA.

(a) Sun Conjunction Mars in Leo

On August 8, 1923 a conjunction of Sun and Mars took place in Leo 15.19. The point is to determine the locality where the extreme heat indicated by this conjunction would develop maximum intensity. For this purpose, we transposed the figure for the previous new Moon on July 14, 0:41 a.m. Greenwich and noted that the hot, dry sign Leo (calorific in nature) occupied the lower meridian from Toulouse, France and covering geographical areas approximately 30 degrees eastward. Furthermore, Mars was fractionally more than two degrees west of Toulouse, with both conjoined luminaries applying to a conjunction. This was indicative of drought and extreme high temperatures. These reached a cumulative point at the Sun-Mars conjunction in Leo on August 8. On August 9, in Toulouse, unprecedented temperatures (111° in the shade) were reported in the news items.

Meanwhile, in the United States opposite extremes of temperatures and weather were in evidence. At Scott's Bluff, Neb., a snow flurry climaxed two weeks of rainy and cold weather. The same lunation map, transposed to the longitude of Scott's Bluff, shows Saturn on the upper meridian four degrees west of that locale, very clearly indicative of the condensation of aqueous vapors and lower ranges of temperature as the Sun formed a sextile aspect to Saturn close to that meridian.

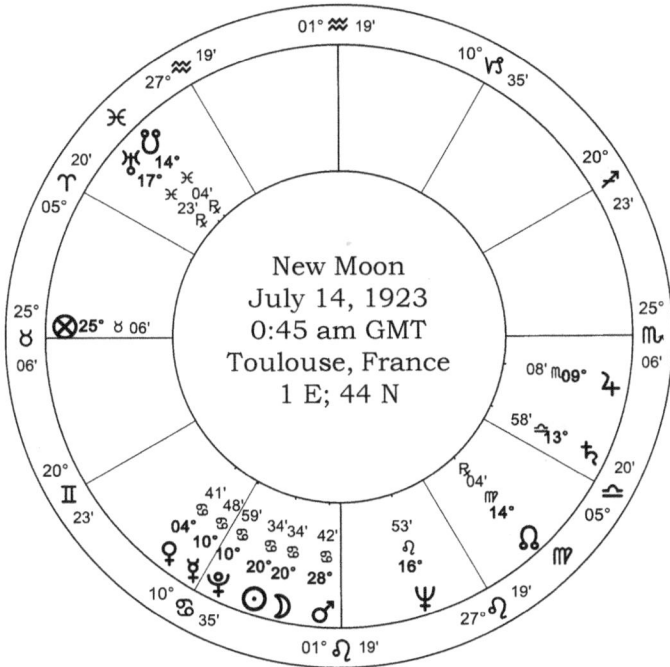

New Moon
July 14, 1923
0:45 am GMT
Toulouse, France
1 E; 44 N

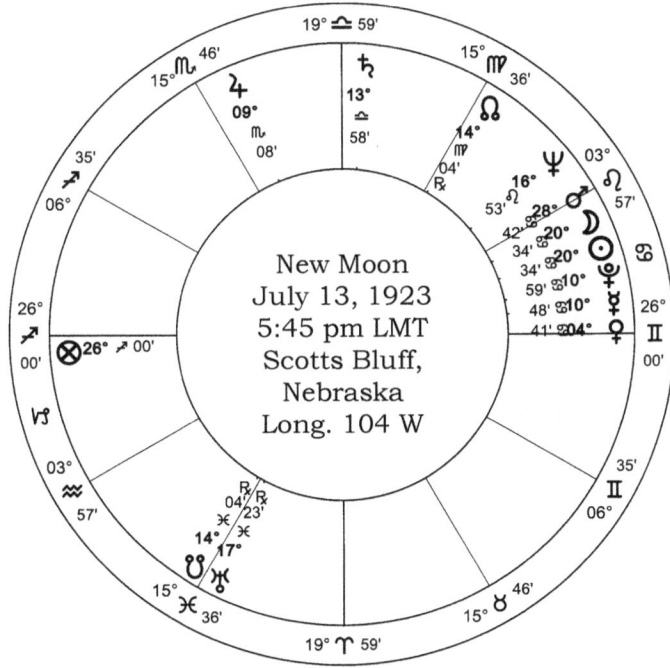

New Moon
July 13, 1923
5:45 pm LMT
Scotts Bluff,
Nebraska
Long. 104 W

During the summer both Mars and Venus were in the North Tropic, indicating spells of heat and humidity, followed by thunderstorms and freak weather when these various bodies formed a conjunction with Neptune.

On August 17, news items reported that the summer of 1923 was intensely hot throughout the United States (G-3.01) and that freak weather including droughts, cloudbursts of record intensity and other peculiar extremes of atmospheric phenomena had occurred in nearly every State except the extreme southwest (note Saturn in the south angle, moderating the heat but inducing cloudiness and rain (G-5). While these extreme differentials of temperatures were affecting various parts of the world, the exponents of the sunspot weather theory were pondering a solution in the front page columns of the New York World dated August 17, 1923.

(b) Mars Conjunction Jupiter: At the Full Moon on July 2, 1928, 7:48 p.m. Denver, (105th meridian), Mars and Jupiter were shown approaching to a conjunction on the lower meridian at 109° west longitude. The actual conjunction, in Taurus 5.00 was not exact until July 4 but the heat wave developed over the Middle West as forecasted and was followed by storms of tornado intensity in the Dakotas and surrounding States, resulting in considerable property damage. (3.04).

(c) Mars in perigee: When Mars reached a station closest to the earth in December, 1928, smallpox was approaching epidemic form in Hartford, Conn. (3.01)

(d) Mars in the North Tropic: Mars reaches extreme north declination at periods of nearly two years. During July, 1936, when Mars was thus stationed, New York established an all-time record of 103 degrees on July 9, 1936. In July, 1938, forest fires leveling vast tracts of forests in Washington State and Vancouver Island, B.C. followed droughts. Based on Mars in the North Tropic with Mars and Sun in conjunction on July 24, we have definitely forecast these fires a year in advance, stating that fires would start from the tops of trees. When official meteorologists blamed campers for the fires, the Washington (D.C.) Daily News, dated July 26, 1938, quoted excerpts from our forecast of this phenomenon. (3.01).

4

JUPITER'S INFLUENCE ON WEATHER

4.01—GENERAL:

JUPITER, the most ponderous planet of our solar system, is 89,109 miles in diameter or 131/3 times the diameter of the Earth and has a sidereal period of 11.86 years. Symbolizing the indigo ray in the solar spectrum, imparting positive electricity and temperate, this major planet normally inclines to promote north winds, an increase of ozone and fair weather cumuli. One of the chief characteristics of the Jupiter influence is to elevate temperature with accompanying rising barometer. Owing to moderate descending air currents, humidity is minimized. If excessively high temperatures prevail at the time of Jupiter's major station or aspects, this is brought about by electrical actions. When Jupiter is close to or attaining its aphelion or apogee stations, its power to increase temperatures is considerably lessened. On the other hand, when in perihelion or perigee higher averages of temperature are induced.

Observations indicate that Jupiter exerts a strong electro-magnetic pull on the earth, that it is instrumental in producing seismic disturbances, and that in combination with the planet Uranus it sets up herzian waves that upset the electro-magnetic conditions of the atmosphere.

Being temperate in nature, Jupiter, though traditionally referred to as the "Preserver", can vary character when configured with other major bodies. For example when with Mars, heat, drought and thunder are induced; when with Saturn, which is negative, excessive humidity, cloudiness and prolonged atmospheric depressions are observed; when with Uranus, sudden abnormal high pressure areas, low ranges of temperature, high wind velocity to extremes up to 90 miles per hour, magnetic storms and peculiar health conditions arising from chills; when with Neptune, excessive humidity, stagnant conditions of the atmosphere, higher ranges of temperature, freak storms and pandemic diseases. Seismic phenomena.

47

When Jupiter is in the equator, the north Tropic, near its perihelion station in the sign Aries, also when stationary, or forming conjunction or sextile aspect with the Sun, rising temperatures with accompanying generation of ozone that makes the atmosphere comfortable and invigorating. This is the sort of warm weather that farmers refer to as "growing weather."

In charts of solar ingresses or eclipses, note particularly those points in geographical longitude where Jupiter occupies the lower meridian for generally fine weather and good crops in season, provided, of course, that other major bodies as above referred to, do not conflict with this position. Jupiter on the meridian also indicates susceptibility to seismic disturbances when the planet Mars either transits or forms magnetic aspects to the degree held by Jupiter. Weatherwise, Jupiter should be the favorite of all who indulge in outdoor sports or activities; or the expectant bride who hopes for a fair wedding day is recommended to set a day when the Sun is in conjunction or in 60 degree angle with Jupiter.

4.02—Primary Stations, Jupiter: SUNSPOTS:

With reference to Jupiter's perihelion station in Aries, when a minor cycle of sunspot activity follows, and the aphelion station or opposite point in longitude where the period of minimum sunspot activity normally coincides, Rudolf Mewes, a German scientist, issued a noteworthy brochure in 1901 in which he pointed out that the great solar period of sunspots is produced by the actions of the planets Jupiter, Saturn and Uranus approximately every 111 years. The cycle does not culminate exactly at that time but measures to 111 years as a focal point because ten cycles of Jupiter (11.86 years each), four cycles of Saturn (29.4 years each) and one-and-a-half cycles of the 84 year period of Uranus converge near that time. He also stressed an intermediate cycle of sunspot activity at 55 years, equivalent to five periods of Jupiter and two of Saturn, accounting not only for great periods of drought, epidemic diseases and changes in mass human psychology, but actually predicting the period of the first World War—between 1910 and 1920! He also stressed the importance of 28 year cycles as those influencing minor deluges coincidental with flourishing times in art and science and that the greater the intensity of sunspots in drought epochs, the more likelihood of warlike activities. A period of maximum intensity culminates at cycles of 1351 years when multiples of the periodic revolutions of the three major planets mentioned bring them all together in conjunction near the same point in longitude.

In this respect, it is noteworthy to mention that both Jupiter and Saturn form successive conjunctions with each other and with Uranus in the zodiacal sign Taurus during 1941-1942, thus concentrating their combined influences for major intensity of electro-magnetic phenomena, abnormal weather and for affecting the mass psychology. And the world appears to be reacting to the major cycle of greatest intensity. As to effects on weather and seismic disturbances, manifestations should speak for themselves.

4.03—JUPITER WITH SATURN:

Jupiter and Saturn form their conjunction in one of the "earth" signs every twenty years, the last conjunction having occurred on February 15, 1941, 1:11 a.m., L.M.T., Washington, D.C., in Taurus 9° 07' 28". The previous cyclic conjunction took place on September 9, 1921, 11:07 p.m., L.M.T., Washington, D.C. The oppositions happen midway between two such periods. On December 20, 1945 Jupiter, in Libra 23.15 will form its quadrature to Saturn in Cancer 23.15. Owing to the fact that these major planets move so slowly in their orbits and accordingly their configurations with each other are very slow in forming and separating, the aspects thus formed by conjunction, opposition or square are observed not only to upset the weather for months at a time but also to indicate very definite effects on economic trends. Jupiter typifies expansion; Saturn relates to contraction. Downfall under these configurations ranges higher than the normal average and health conditions are affected, which was amply verified following the conjunction in February, 1941, as well as immediately preceding the phenomenon, when grippe was prevalent due to <u>predominating dampness</u>. In proper growing seasons such weather conditions affect fruits (Jupiter) particularly. Judgment should be regulated by the sign positions of the respective significators and their angles to the earth over certain geographic meridians in solar ingress charts.

With reference to public health under these configurations, sunshine is deficient. Prolonged periods of cloudiness induce predominating dampness which wears down the body's resistance. Blood pressure becomes low. Diseases spread from east to west or from lowlands to highlands. When Jupiter forms such aspects from Scorpio, volcanic activity may be expected. In Taurus, then seismic phenomena follows periodically. Since Jupiter is the general significator of life insurance (money house of 8th sign), leading insurance companies might advantageously review sickness and mortality statistics for those years when negative configurations of Jupiter and Saturn are operating, also comparing years of perihelion stations with those of Jupiter's aphelion.

The positive sextile, trine, semi-sextile or 150 degree angles between these major bodies incline to lower ranges of temperature for the season, but with less affect on downfall.

4.04—JUPITER WITH URANUS:

Since both Jupiter and Uranus incline to high barometric pressure and induce descending air currents from the higher levels of the atmosphere, their configurations are conducive to high velocity winds, low ranges of temperature for the season, electro-magnetic disturbances and peculiar conditions of health resulting from sudden extreme changes in the atmosphere.

The conjunction, square and opposition configurations are of primary importance in this respect, and likewise the parallel of declination. At such periods, the state of the weather is generally disturbed, the electrical condition of the air is affected, sunspot activity increases and displays of the Aurora Borealis become more frequent and brighter than usual. The strong magnetic fields and the discharges that are sent out from the disturbed surface of the Sun coincide with configurations of Jupiter with Uranus or other major planets. An increase of such phenomena is also indicated when Jupiter attains its perihelion station.

The Aurora Borealis or "Northern Lights" appears in the upper layers of the earth's atmosphere where the air is very rarified, where wind velocities are greatest and where helium, the lightest known gas, prevails. It is in these higher levels that the configurations of Uranus generate descending air currents and maximum negative electricity, whereas Jupiter relates to positive electricity. The combinations of these two major bodies create static conditions in the atmosphere that scientists so frequently ascribe to sunspots.

For example, on May 14, 1921, a manifestation of the Aurora Borealis—magnetic storms—disturbed telegraphic communications and caused considerable annoyances wherever electrical communications were being employed. Scientists, according to press reports, were unable to explain the phenomenon. The fact remains, however, that exactly on that date Jupiter formed an opposition to the planet Uranus. The conjunction of Jupiter and Uranus in Aries 0° 25' while both bodies were in the same parallel of declination on January 25, 1928, indicated similar magnetic disturbances in the atmosphere. On January 31, 1938 Uranus, in Taurus 9° 48', was squared by Jupiter from Aquarius 9° 48'. This last mentioned configuration was intensified by Sun conjunction Jupiter and square Uranus during the two days preceding and by Venus forming the same configurations on the very day of the major conjunction. And on that day an earthquake was felt at Honolulu. Observations have indicated that weather was greatly disturbed at the time of each conjunction, opposition or square between Jupiter and Uranus, that temperatures declined, that wind velocities increased, that magnetic disturbances manifested and that seismic disturbances increased, both in frequency and intensity. The deduction is obvious concerning effects of the conjunction of these major bodies on May 7, 1941, in Taurus 25° 38' and with four other heavenly bodies in Taurus making a very rare array of conjunctions with those two major planets up to and including May 20. A period of maximum intensity should develop on May 11 when the New Moon in Scorpio 20° 13' brings all those forces to concentrative operation. Anticipated effects of this major conjunction were commented on in Astrotech, March 21, 1941, p. 24. In statistical data on pages immediately following, we will include reports concerning effects of this conjunction and previous configurations between Jupiter and Uranus.

In terms of the chart for the Vernal Equinox, March 21, 1941, 12h. 21m. p.m., the conjunction of Jupiter and Uranus falls on the lower meridian at Long. 47⁰ E. Points adjacent to that meridian and eastward should experience the greatest atmospheric and magnetic disturbances. Secondary points should culminate at 137 E., 43 W. and Long. 133 West.

The parallel of declination should be interpreted in terms of the relative declinations. If declination of one should be south and the other north, effects would be similar to opposition. If both be in the same direction of declination the effects of the conjunction are judged. The parallel of these bodies on May 20, 1941 is equally as potent as the conjunction.

It is futile to attempt accurate day to day weather forecasts under the negative aspects of Jupiter and Uranus, since they incline to erratic extremes of atmospheric and magnetic conditions and their influences may also be prolonged owing to the slow motion of these bodies.

In Pearce's Textbook of Astrology, statistical data is presented in support of the statement that the conjunctions of Jupiter and Uranus (and likewise their oppositions), owing to their effects upon the electrical state of the atmosphere, have almost invariably been attended by disturbed health conditions.

4.05—JUPITER WITH NEPTUNE:

Configurations between Jupiter and Neptune incline to milder temperatures than the average for the season, though inducing sudden changes and breezy spasms. The positive sextile, trine, 30 and 150 degree angles are conducive to mild, pleasant weather since Neptune is the higher octave expression of Venus. Atmospheric conditions are similar to those of Jupiter-Venus but are comparatively more sudden. In the summer months peculiar atmospheric conditions develop over limited geographical areas along the lowlands. These may range from sultry warm atmosphere to night hazes which are finally dissipated by local thunderstorms or squalls. Wind direction is likely to be variable and of low velocity, with peculiar calms preceding local squalls from the west. In cooler seasons fogs, especially at night.

The conjunction, opposition, square, semi square and 135 degree aspects between Jupiter and Neptune appear to affect the atmosphere as the results of volcanic dust arising from volcanic eruptions and which may remain in the air for long periods. This applies particularly to the conjunction, opposition and parallel of declination. These major configurations are epidemic breeders and the conjunctions have been observed to intensify seismic phenomena.

4.06—Statistical Data - JUPITER: EARTHQUAKES:

Although earthquakes follow upon the heels of solar eclipses, the relative positions of the major planets to certain geographic meridians are the motivating factors rather than the eclipse. From such positions are inferred the specific areas likely to be affected.

(a) The accompanying map of the heavens for actual moment of the severe earthquake in Los Angeles, Calif., on March 10, 1933 reveals nothing precise in itself to explain the phenomenon. But if we revert back to the solar eclipse on August 31, 1932, 2:45 pm., E.S.T. that was visible in the United States, this chart, transposed to the longitude of Los Angeles reveals Jupiter and Neptune conjoined with the luminaries on the upper meridian, hence indicating the geographical point of greatest magnetic pull. The next point was to determine the time when tremors might be expected. In the eclipse chart, Neptune occupied Virgo 7.45 and the eclipse fell in Virgo 8.11. The accompanying chart shows that Mars (excitement) was transiting the magnetic field set up by Jupiter and Neptune at the

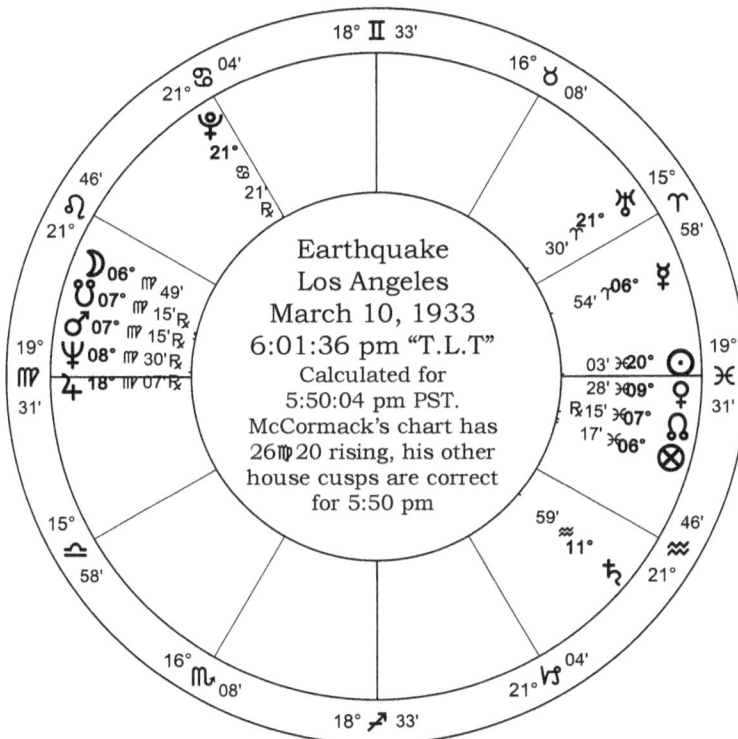

Chart center text:

Earthquake
Los Angeles
March 10, 1933
6:01:36 pm "T.L.T"
Calculated for
5:50:04 pm PST.
McCormack's chart has
26♍20 rising, his other
house cusps are correct
for 5:50 pm

time of the preceding eclipse, the rising Moon also indicating the tidal factor in the same area. An interesting point to observe is that both the Moon and Mars at the time of the seismic disturbance were also transiting a point within an exact semi-square angle (45 degrees) of Pluto. The Sun, which actually set at 6:04 p.m. L.M.T., was two degrees past the opposition with Jupiter. Jupiter was exactly squaring the meridian at Los Angeles when the earthquake originated.

Charleston, S.C. Earthquake:

A solar eclipse of the Sun on August 29, 1886, 7:34 a.m., Long. 79.56 W. and Lat. 32.47 N. fell in Virgo 6.04, when the midheaven was Cancer 1.13 and the Ascendant was Libra 1.07. Jupiter and Uranus were then within a degree of conjunction in the ascendant. On August 31, 1886 a severe earthquake occurred at Charleston, S.C. A. J. Pearce, in his Zadkiel's Almanac for 1885, coordinating testimonies at the time of the eclipse with those in the chart for the conjunction of Mars and Jupiter, June 27, 1886, 5:30 a.m., Washington, D.C., definitely foretold the time, place and character of this earthquake with amazing accuracy. Pearce's Textbook of

Astrology is replete with statistical data bearing upon similar long range forecasts during many years of profound astrotechnical researches.

(b) JUPITER-URANUS: EXTREMES OF WEATHER AND MAGNETIC STORMS:

On May 13, 1921, Jupiter, in Virgo 9.00, opposed Uranus. An unusual display of the Aurora Borealis was reported and cables burned out mysteriously.

On July 15, 1927, Jupiter (direct) and Uranus (retrograde) formed a conjunction in Aries 3° 24' and three inches of rainfall within 24 hours was recorded at New York City. After Jupiter turned retrograde, these bodies formed a second conjunction on August 11, 1927, in Aries 3.00. Temperatures were below normal average throughout August and were accompanied by excessive downfall. The English Channel had one of the worst summers in its history. The New York Weather Bureau forecasters reported that in all the history of the local Weather Bureau dating its records from 1871, there had not been such an August as that of 1927. During that month the average temperature was 5 degrees below normal and it was the coldest August on record. Rain, rain and more rain was reported throughout the Northern Hemisphere.

(c) On January 25, 1928, Jupiter and Uranus were conjoined in Aries 0° 25' while both planets were in the same parallel of declination. Mercury was then forming a semi-square (45° angles with the conjoined bodies. During the noon hour a wind velocity of 80 miles an hour was officially reported in New York City, but unofficial reports from suburbs contended that velocities ranging up to 90 miles per hour had been recorded. Thousands of large store windows were blown in and many large display advertising signs were blown down.

(d) PERIHELION OF JUPITER:

Since Jupiter attains its perihelion station in Aries at periods of 11.86 years, Dr. Luke Broughton, in his "Elements of Astrology" presents statistical data concerning these recurring cycles from 1797 in order to show how they are related to the spread of epidemic diseases. He quotes the New York Medical Journal for 1871, (August) in which it was pointed out that cholera had broken out in Hudwar, India every twelfth year since 1783, and notably in 1867. Broughton carried this analysis further to show a similar prevalence of cholera near the central point of Jupiter's perihelion in 1892-93, particularly in Germany, France, Russia, Spain and Italy. He also pointed out the prevalence of typhus fever during 1881 and 1892 in New York, when Jupiter on both occasions was in perihelion. It was noted that many cloudbursts, cyclones and earthquakes accompanied these phenomena.

(e) AURORAS, HURRICANES AND SEISMIC ACTIVITY: JUPITER SQUARE URANUS

On January 31, 1938, Jupiter, in Aquarius 9° 48', squared Uranus in Taurus 9° 48'. This configuration was intensified by the Sun's conjunction with Jupiter in Aquarius and square to Jupiter during the two days preceding and by Venus forming similar angles with these bodies on the exact date of their conjunction. It may be pertinent to mention that Uranus had attained a stationary position in Taurus 9.43 on January 18, as Jupiter approached close to the square. On the 17th, the Moon had left the opposition of Jupiter from Leo 6.29 and was squaring Uranus. Frigid arctic currents descended upon the Eastern States over January 18, sending temperatures down to zero at New York City, 16 below at Albany and 42 below in the Quebec Province. Wire communications throughout Canada were disrupted by magnetic storms.

From that date on, magnetic storms increased in intensity. On January 20, a sunspot estimated to have an area of 3,500,000,000 square miles and one of the largest seen since the Royal Observatory began keeping records in 1875, was reported clearly visible with the aid of glasses in London. (N. Y. Sun, Jan. 20, 1938).

On January 23, the Coast and Geodetic Survey reported that a "very severe magnetic storm" beginning at 12:30 a.m. E.S.T., disrupted short wave radio transmission completely. The report said that the reason for such storms was not fully understood, but that they usually accompany the appearance of large sunspots. (N. Y. Sun, Jan. 23, 1938).

Worst quake in 11 years rocks Hawaii (Headline, N.Y. Times, Jan. 23, 1938).

London, Jan 26, 1938: (Quoting item from N. Y. Post of that date) "It was not the end of the world. It was not a new war. It was not a fire ..... By press, radio and telephone, officials explained that the aurora, rarely seen in Southern or Western Europe, was caused by an electrical disturbance on the Sun's surface.... The lights were seen clearly in Italy, Spain, Portugal and even southernmost

Gibraltar, Austria, Switzerland, the Netherlands and the British Isles. Telephone systems were tied up in some parts of France. Short wave radio between London and New York was disrupted."

London, Jan. 29: Winds which at times reached ninety miles and hour—hurricane force—raked the British Isles today, spreading property damage, disrupting sea travel. Rain, sleet and hail were borne by the raging winds. Scotland was the region hardest hit. (N. Y. Herald Tribune, Jan. 30, 1938).

During this same period over the Eastern States, a Newark-to-Washington air-transport, caught in an 80 mile gale, was blown back to Hartford, Conn.

These phenomena were definitely explained and their time and character predicted by us in printed circulars publicly circulated and dated December 11, 1937. The motivating causes were then ascribed to the combined actions of the planets Jupiter and Uranus which were to form an angle of 90 degrees to each other in longitude on January 31, 1938. These observations were reiterated by astrologers in a public lecture entitled "Refining Astrological Methods" delivered before the Astrologers' Guild of America, in New York City, on December 16, 1937.

(f) JUPITER CONJUNCTION URANUS, TAURUS 25° 38', May 7, 1941:
The effects of these conjunctions are prolonged and manifest periodically, when excited by accompanying phenomena. Due to foreign news censorship resulting from the European war situation, records of unusual weather phenomena fail to reach this country from abroad. On May 16, the Sun formed a parallel with both Jupiter and Uranus, thus engendering their combined influences. From Columbus, Ohio, on that date, news dispatches reported that cyclonic winds caused considerable property damage in Central Ohio. Airport observers said that gales reaching a velocity of 80 miles per hour were recorded.

At Chicago, Ill, winds blowing 75 miles per hour destroyed 40 airplanes, blew down four hangars, shattered windows, wrecked many hundreds of chimneys and left many outlying highways blocked by fallen trees during a thunderstorm in the Chicago area. At Kendallville, Ind., following a heavy wind storm during the night, power lines were blown down. Resultant power failure closed factories. Roofs of ten buildings damaged. Trees were uprooted.

On the same date, at Pasadena, Calif., 6:37:25 p.m. P.S.T., a very strong earthquake, estimated to be 6,000 miles away, direction undetermined, was recorded.

(g) SUNSPOTS AND MAGNETIC STORMS:

It is now stated by scientists that ultra-violet light (actinic rays) and electrons descending from the upper strata of atmosphere ionize the air surrounding the surface of the earth. Ionization, they say, is a process of wrecking molecules. Bits of molecules are torn away electrons. Whereupon the hulks that remain are in a tremendous state of electrical agitation.

Three well known layers of electrification are produced by solar electrons. One lies at a height of sixty miles, a second at about 120 miles and a third at 180 miles. Were it not for these layers, radio waves would be cast off in straight lines into space like mud from a turning wheel. As it is, the waves flash to the mirror-like layers, back to earth. The lower layer reflects the fairly long radio waves, next the shorter waves and the highest the very short waves.

When sunspots are numerous not only are these mirrors in the sky affected, so that radio communication becomes impossible, but the magnetism of the earth as well. We have what we call a magnetic storm, which has no relation, however, to storms of rain, thunder and lightning.

Magnetic storms are most intense in polar regions and are generally accompanied by auroral displays. (Astrometeorologists have pointed out that positive electricity is strongest at the earth's equator (heat) and that negative electricity reaches maximum at the poles—cold). A pronounced tendency of the earth's magnetism to vary at intervals of 26 to 28 days, approximately the period of the Moon's revolution around the earth as well as the Sun's rotation on its axis supports the theory that sunspots which rotate with these phenomena are not directly due to the solar atmosphere itself but to the Moon's configurations with the same point in celestial longitude (as will be noted by either Sun or Moon in conjunction, square or opposition to positions of major planets when they form their major configurations). In this connection, minor fourteen and seven day periods are of interest.

The aurora curtain is about 60 to 70 miles above the earth and never lower than 27 miles. That which the exponents of astroscience ascribe to the planets as vibratory influences is explained by physicists as a state of electrical agitation. But there is a wide differential in results depending on whether <u>negative</u> or <u>positive</u> electrical agitation is in preponderance. The stronger influence of negative electricity induces magnetic action while the greater generation of positive electricity induces heat and manifestation of lightning flashes, accompanied by rising air currents at the point of observations meeting negative currents at higher altitudes. In winter months, warmer currents prevail in higher altitudes. At 46,260 feet temperatures of 74 above have been registered while ground temperatures were 23 below zero! This record was reported from Fairbanks, Alaska, Feb. 17, 1938.

5

SATURN'S INFLUENCE ON WEATHER

5.01—GENERAL:
"Shall it not utterly wither when the east wind toucheth it?"
—Ezekiel XVII, 10.

SATURN, with a diameter of 78,714 miles, is next in size to the ponderous planet Jupiter. Its mass is about 985 times the contents of the Earth. This planet completes a revolution of its orbit in about 29½ years or 10,759.22 days. The influence of Saturn is exactly opposite in character to that of Jupiter and Mars. Imparting negative electricity, the rays of this planet have a tendency to lower the temperature and barometer, induce winds from the east, promote humidity, clouds and condense aqueous vapors. Under positive or harmonious angles, gradual but definitely <u>lower ranges of temperature</u> with generally fair weather. The conjunction, parallel, opposition, square and semi-square increase putrefaction through <u>dampness</u> and obscured sunshine, hence the proverbial "shadows of Saturn."

Blue and gray rays predominate under Saturn's dominion—the blue for cold and their combination with grays for depressants. Prolonged easterly winds under Saturn's influence are contrary to the Earth's normal rotation on its axis from west to east. This celestial body <u>concentrates the influence of the sign</u> in which it may be posited at any time, which may be amply verified by observing when the Sun forms a conjunction and parallel with Saturn in the successive signs. It is a matter of official records that the record high temperature of 102 degrees on August 6, 1918 occurred when the Sun formed a conjunction with Saturn in Leo and that the heat wave was not broken until the Sun parallel Saturn was formed. On February 6, 1934, when Sun and Saturn formed a conjunction in <u>Aquarius</u>, a record low temperature of 14° degrees below zero was officially recorded in Washington, D.C. Leo is the sign of <u>calcination</u> and Aquarius is indicative of <u>crystallization</u>. In the southern hemisphere these signatures are reversed.

Atmospheric conditions resulting from influences of Saturn's rays are slow in developing and in waning, hence the prolonged intensity of the northeasters along the coasts with their corresponding cold waves in the interior. Saturn weather is always penetrating. It does not follow that storms will develop over the point of observation on the very date of a Saturn configuration. The low pressure areas advance eastward against the wind which may blow from the east for hours. The position of Saturn in the preceding ingress chart, together with the transiting Moon through the upper or lower meridian or squares thereto afford definite timing points at the place of observation, as we will endeavor to illustrate under statistical data.

5.02—PRIMARY STATIONS:
When Saturn crosses the equator, (as in the spring of 1938), or the north Tropics (as during the summer of 1915 and June and July, 1944), when stationary, occupying the upper or lower meridian in ingress or lunar quarter charts, or when forming adverse configurations including conjunction with the Sun or planets of positive electrical nature, the atmosphere is greatly disturbed. Humidity is then excessive in the lowlands and cold is more intense in the higher altitudes of the interior. Inundations coincide with the perigee and perihelion stations of Saturn which recur at periods of approximately 29½ years. Occupying the lower meridian at a solar quarter, retarded sunshine, prevailing dampness, downfall and temperatures below seasonal average retard crops. In cooler months this position induces heavy frosts, especially in higher altitudes of the interior. Coldest winters prevail when Saturn occupies the signs Capricorn and Aquarius. Ice and snow remain long. Easterly winds and dust particles (carbon) preponderate under Saturn's negative rays and colder weather sets in after low pressure areas have passed eastward of the point of observation. In winter months, the mild humid atmosphere that precedes the approach of these storms with accompanying easterly winds, or southeast, is one of the chief danger signals. As applied to weather, Saturn and saturation are synonymous in character of expression.

5.03—SATURN WITH URANUS:
Owing to the slow motions of Saturn and Uranus in their orbits, the effects of their configurations endure for months. The conjunction, parallel, opposition and 90 degree angles are all conducive to prolonged disturbed atmospheric conditions, with

temperatures below the normal average for the season. These indications are intensified where either Saturn or Uranus occupies the meridian, thus indicating geographically an originating point of such phenomena in the atmosphere. Saturn thus placed causes low pressure areas and precipitation above normal. Uranus in similar stations induces high pressure areas and abnormally low temperatures for the season. Judgment regarding the <u>latitudinal</u> paths of such phenomena should be governed by the north or south angles of the planets in relation to the equinox or solstice maps. Similarly when either planet occupies the east or west angles of the ingress charts and forms exact squares to the meridian, other originating points of weather abnormalities may be determined geographically. It follows, therefore, that geographical meridians 90 degrees apart in longitude are focal points where the planets register maximum electro-magnetic attractions on the earth. The conditions then trace courses eastward round the globe.

For example: On October 1, 1918 Saturn, in Leo 24° 14' opposed Uranus in Aquarius 24° 14'. Epidemics of influenza had already begun in August, coinciding with Sun's conjunction with Saturn followed by its opposition to Uranus. Subsequent peaks of intensity were indicated during October and November under the squares and again in February, 1919 when the Sun conjoined Uranus in Aquarius and opposed Saturn. Many cases of Asiatic cholera were reported from Europe during that year. Continued extremes of weather all other the world at that time were ascribed to heavy and continued cannonading on the European battlefronts prior to the signing of the World War Armistice in November, 1918.

Observations over many years seem to indicate that when the slowest moving major planets are adversely configured, electrical conditions in the atmosphere are disturbed, sudden and extreme variations of temperature and weather incline to lower the body resistance. Pandemic disease spreads from <u>east to west</u> round the globe, in the opposite direction to normal movements of weather phenomena. Abnormal frequency of easterly and northeasterly winds under these Saturn-Uranus combinations, accompanied by continued <u>deficiency of sunshine</u>, in the opinion of astro-meteorologists, result chiefly from such unusual planetary phenomena. These atmospheric conditions appear to be associated with the <u>absence or deficiency of positive electricity in the atmosphere</u>.

Saturn and Uranus will form a conjunction in Taurus 29° 20'

(fixed sign) on May 3, 1942. As this conjunction falls directly on the place of Alcyone in the Pleiades, it may be of research interest to seismologists. The last conjunction of those major celestial bodies happened on January 5, 1897. It is amusing when we overhear people say "We don't experience the old fashioned winters we had when I was a child." The trends of weather, however, usually repeat themselves when the cycles are effective.

With reference to Saturn square Uranus, the Winter Solstice map for December 22, 1930, 8:40 a.m., 75th meridian showed Scorpio 12.00 on the Midheaven and Capricorn 12:23 on the eastern horizon. Saturn was tenanted exactly on the ascendant in Capricorn 12.36 and formed the exact square to Uranus in Aries on December 12,1930. However, please note that the Sun squared Uranus on January 2, 1931, conjoined Saturn on January 5 and on the following day opposed Jupiter. The planet Jupiter had opposed Saturn on January 10. Those first ten days of January brought planetary indications to focus.

A news item in the New York Times of January 25, 1931 reported 1,185 influenza cases in New York City during the week as against 918 in the previous week. Pneumonia cases totaled 1,239 against a total of 1,097 the previous week. Total cases of pneumonia then reported were 3,286, with 1,349 pneumonia deaths. Up to that time influenza cases totaled 2,724. An item in the N. Y. Herald Tribune, of same date, quoted an Associated Press dispatch from Tokyo stating that influenza hit 486,000 persons in Tokyo, where police distributed pamphlets urging the population to don masks.

When scientists are unable to trace effects to causes they conveniently refer to them as "acts of God." These planets previously formed their conjunction in Taurus in July, 1851 and again in March, 1852.

5.04—SATURN WITH NEPTUNE:
When the planets Saturn and Neptune are in conjunction, opposition, quadrature or semi-square aspect to each other abnormal atmospheric conditions may be expected to endure for weeks and sometimes months at a time. Greatest extremes have been indicated under the conjunctions and oppositions. Both planets are very slow in motion. Since Saturn may conjoin and pass Neptune and, after attaining a stationary position in celestial longitude, turn retrograde and later move direct again, the same configurations can recur repeatedly. Consequently unusual extremes of weather may affect

extensive geographical areas through an entire year. In the Spring season the combined influence of these planets conduces to low mists by day and abnormal fogs by night. The atmosphere inclines to excessive saturation of the air and diffused sunshine. In Summer, peculiar hazes, devitalizing atmosphere, and precipitation is heavier than the average. Saturn and Neptune are similar to Saturn and Venus in effects, though more extreme. In Autumn, excessive cloudiness with heavy night frosts. In Winter, temperatures range below the normal and excessive downfall of snow snarls and impedes traffic.

An illustration was the conjunction of Saturn and Neptune in Leo 5.00 during August, 1917 as Saturn was moving direct in geocentric longitude. After turning retrograde in December, Saturn attained a stationary position in Leo 7.37 on April 9, 1918, in close parallel with Neptune in Leo 4⁰19'. Weather conditions throughout the world were greatly disturbed during the winter of 1917-1918, temperatures were abnormally low and downfall of snow was not only in excess of normal but remained frozen at considerable depth throughout the winter in Eastern States particularly. Atmospheric conditions had a devitalizing effect on public health. Epidemics of spinal meningitis, infantile paralysis, influenza and grippe caused grave concern to the health authorities.

It is noteworthy to mention that while a record low temperature of 13 degrees below zero was recorded at New York City on December 30, 1917, with recurring extreme low temperatures in February (with Uranus in Aquarius as a contributing factor), a record high temperature of 103 degrees was registered at New York City on August 6, 1918 when the Sun formed a parallel of declination with Saturn in Leo. Where configurations between the slowest motioned major planets are concerned, due consideration should be given to the nature of the signs in which the planets may be posited. For example: On January 18, 1937 the planet Saturn, in Pisces 18° 45', opposed Neptune in Virgo 18° 45'. In the chart for the Winter Solstice on December 21, 1936, 7:18 p.m. L.M.T., Washington, D.C., (as illustrated under paragraph 3.01) Saturn occupied the upper meridian at Long. 112 W. in close opposition to Neptune which was posited on the nadir at 110 W. Meanwhile, the calorific Mars on the lower meridian at Washington induced higher ranges of temperature from that meridian eastward and with comparatively less precipitation over the Eastern States. Observing the Saturn-Neptune combination affecting the western areas of the country, we wrote to Neal O'Hara, columnist for the New York Post, on December 19,

1936, expressing the opinion that this planetary combination would be hazardous for aviation between the Pacific Coast and Denver and indicated that ice might form on wings of airplanes in transit. This interpretation was subsequently confirmed and was duly credited by the columnist after a series of aviation disasters attributed to the cause described.

Illustrating further, how various geographical areas respond differently according to the planets in direct angle to places of observation, it will be seen that midway between Washington, D.C. where Mars occupied the lower meridian and Long. 110 W. where Neptune occupied the nadir is the 93rd meridian as the focal point where these influences converged geographically. And it was exactly in this geographical area where the disastrous floods of the Missouri and Mississippi Rivers wreaked their greatest devastation during January, 1937. It is also our opinion, based on previous observations of negative Saturn-Neptune configurations, that these phenomena are related to and followed by greatest rises in the rate of mortality from infantile paralysis. (Neptune, glandular system; Saturn, congestions and depression). On July 2, 1944, Saturn, in Cancer 1° 34' (North Tropic) will form a quadrature with Neptune in Libra 1° 34' (Equator). Owing to the cardinal points held by both major bodies and the fact that the Sun conjoins Saturn and squares Neptune at the Summer Solstice of June, 1944, excessive downfall and general extremes of weather during that summer will promise a very disappointing season for the outdoor amusement resorts. Such a configuration by these major bodies from the North Tropic and Equator is indeed a rarity.

Favorable aspects: The sextile, trine, semi-sextile and 150 degree configurations between Saturn and Neptune are conducive to misty and dull atmosphere in the lowlands but showery and cooler weather in the interior and higher altitudes when the place of either planet is excited by transits of other bodies.

5.05—STATISTICAL DATA - SATURN:
(a) Saturn in North Tropic: The accompanying chart is calculated for the Summer solstice of June 22, 1915, when Saturn's station in the north tropic disturbed the weather throughout the summer season. Predominating easterly winds, cloudiness, and excessive rainfall with accompanying low average of temperatures, particularly at weekends when the Moon was in the Equator or the North Tropic, resulted in a very disappointing season for the beaches and outdoor amusement resorts. The moist, changeable Moon in the lower

21° ♈ 29'

27° ♉ 57'
20° ♓ 09'

♂ 20° ♉ 10'
♃ 27° ♓ 22'

♀ 07° ♊ 52'

☉ 00° ♋ ...   25° ♒ 07'

43'   ♊   ♋
03'

♄ 01° ♋ 00'
☿ 05° ♋ 41'
07° ♋ 06'
07° ♋ 07' ℞

℞56' ≈19° ☊
℞16' ≈15° ♅

04° ♌ 27'   04° ♒ 27'

Ψ 29° ♋ 02'

**Summer Solstice
June 22 1915
7:21 am LMT
75W 40N**

☊ 19° ♌ 56' ℞

25° ♌ 07'

15' ♏
29°

47' ♎ 24°   03° ♑ 43'

⊗ 27° ♏ 57'

20° ♍ 09'   ☽

21° ♎ 29'

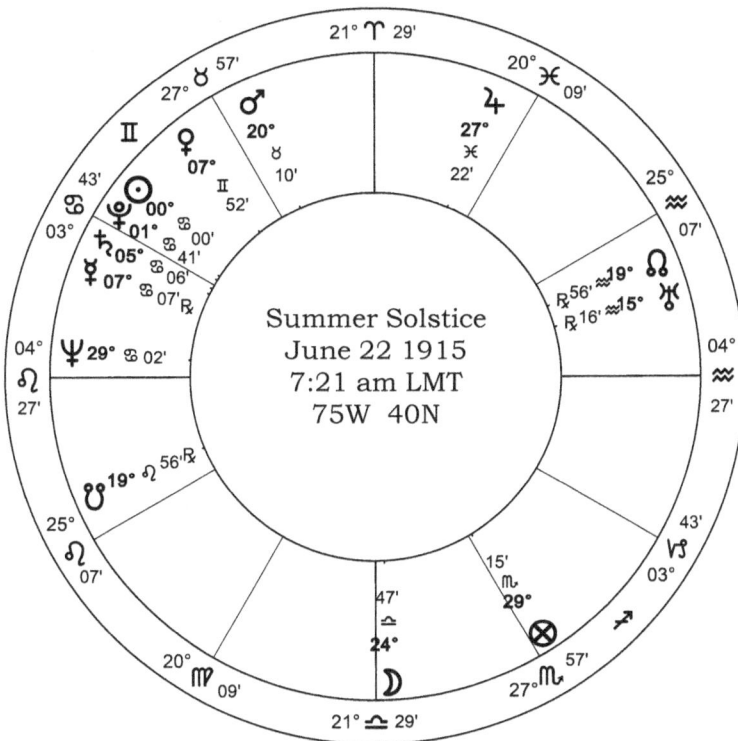

meridian, and squaring Neptune in Cancer, accentuated this condition but Saturn in the North Tropic, squaring the meridian at Long. 91 W., clouded and dampened weather from that point eastward. The entire northern hemisphere was affected by these phenomena as low pressure areas traced their courses eastward. Saturn's characteristic tendency to promote easterly winds and generally dull weather was amply verified during that summer season. Note repetition of this cycle during late June and early July, 1944. (Refer 5.02).

(b) Saturn in south Tropic: During mid-December, 1929, Saturn attained declination 22° 39' S, in the cold sign Capricorn. At the winter Solstice, Dec. 22, 2:45 a.m., L.M.T., Washington, D.C., the Sun was applying to a conjunction with Saturn. At New York City on December 23 1.5 inches of snow gave the first white Christmas since 1919. The number of cloudy days, 17, had been exceeded previously but twice in records for the month of December. During January, 1930, the local weather bureau at New York City recorded 22 cloudy days. (Refer 5.02).

(c) <u>Saturn in the Equator</u>: Saturn was stationary in the equator on December 1, 1937, 4:54 p.m., E.S.T. Mercury squared this position on Dec. 2, 2:24 p.m. A coastal storm moving up the Atlantic Seaboard was pushed eastward to sea accompanied by rain and snow from Cape Hatteras to Sable Island off the coast. Although only light falls of snow were recorded over most of Long Island, <u>2.24 inches were reported at Bermuda</u>. At Kane, Pa., the mercury fell to 8 below zero. On December 3, at Nantucket Lightship a 75 mile per hour gale from the <u>north east</u> was accompanied by driving snow, sleet and mountainous seas. (Refer 5.02).

(d) Saturn <u>stationary</u> and <u>square Uranus</u>: On April 20, 1930, Saturn attained a stationary position in Capricorn 11.53, square Uranus in Aries 12.25. Saturn turned retrograde on the 22nd. Cold weather then developed over the Eastern States, following temperatures of 70 degrees at New York on Easter Sunday, April 20. On April 23, the mercury dropped to 30 degrees at New York City at 6:00 a.m. Freezing temperatures and snowfall in various quantities visited the North Atlantic States, breaking records of fifty years or more. Snow flurries in Washington, a four inch downfall at Saranac Lake, N.Y., with a temperature of 12 degrees. At Pittsburgh, Pa., with a temperature of 27 degrees, frosts damaged fruit and flowers.

It is of interest to note that the lunar quarter on April 20, 1930, 5:09 p.m. E.S.T. showed Cancer 13 on the Midheaven and Libra 11.13 on the ascendant, with <u>Saturn</u> on the <u>lower meridian</u> at Long. 76.00 W. On the 24th, 0:29 a.m., the Moon reached a midway point between Saturn and Uranus when the temperature at New York fell to 29 degrees and a fresh north west wind prevailed.

(e) The lunar quarter charts afford more definite particulars concerning weekly periods, particularly if major planets occupy the upper or lower meridian at or just west of the place of observation.

6

EFFECTS OF THE PLANET URANUS
ON WEATHER

6.01—GENERAL

URANUS, symbolizing cold and negation, is the antithesis of the Sun, the dynamic principle of heat and expansion. As the higher octave expression of the planet Mercury, Uranus emblemizes the actinic red ray in the solar spectrum. Among the elements of the atmosphere, this planet relates to the Heavyside Layer above and beyond the film of ozone surrounding the earth. Imparting negative electricity to the extreme, Uranus induces highest barometric pressure, rapidly declining temperatures and through descending air currents from higher altitudes, conduces to greatest wind velocity. If Mercury is an electrical planet, then Uranus is entitled to recognition as the negative electrical planet par excellence. Impressions by this planet on the weather are sudden, spasmodic and usually extreme. Lower ranges of temperature invariably result from all occupancies of major stations or when configured with Sun or Mercury particularly. The prevailing wind is from the northwest and we have a very good example of this prevailing wind and the accompanying higher wind velocities when the Sun is transiting through the sign Aquarius from January 21 to February 20 annually. Under harmonious aspects, wind veering to northwest clears the atmosphere, the barometer rises fast with correspondingly declining temperatures. Increased wind velocity begins over the higher altitudes of the interior and sweeps downslope to the lowlands. During cold seasons, cold waves, heavy frosts but clear weather, unless contrary planetary rays are operating jointly. Under adverse square, opposition or semi-square configurations (including the conjunction) the atmosphere is cold, overcast, bleak and penetrating. Dark clouds resembling horizontal brushstrokes advancing out of the western sky are harbingers of approaching wind velocity. Lowest temperatures in the history of the Weather Bureau—on December 30, 1917, 13 degrees below zero at New York, and on February 9, 1934, 14 degrees below zero at New York have been indicated respectively by the planets Uranus and Saturn in the cold, electrical sign Aquarius and configured with other celestial bodies in the same sign. During warm seasons, when a period of warm, humid weather precedes the Uranus configurations, violent storms of short duration are followed by a rising barometer and fresh invigorating atmosphere. Temperatures decline most in the highest altitudes, hence mountains and localities in highest elevation respond first to the Uranus positions and configurations.

6.02—MAJOR STATIONS:

Abnormally high barometer with accompanying lower ranges of temperature and wind velocity above the average for the period will accompany the positions of Uranus in the equator (0.00 declination), in extreme north declination, or when stationary (as on January 18, 1938 when a temperature of 16 below zero was reported from Albany, N.Y. and much lower temperatures were recorded in adjacent localities northward). Uranus is potent in the same respects when occupying the lower meridian or when opposing or squaring that point at any geographical point of observation. In maps for solar ingresses into cardinal points, note particularly those geographical areas where Uranus occupies the upper or lower meridian, principally the latter. As a general rule, it will be found that lowest temperatures for the season will prevail and originate in such locales, moving eastward therefrom and changing in character as various electro-magnetic influences of other stellar bodies affect longitudes eastward. Uranus is calculated to attain extreme north declination in March and April, 1950, becoming stationary in the North Tropic on March 10, 1950 (in Cancer 0.56). This last occurred during the summer of 1865. The spring of 1950 should be extremely frigid throughout the northern hemisphere and be attended by peculiar magnetic phenomenon in the upper atmosphere. If Mercury on the meridian is a potential blizzard breeder, Uranus is an extremist in that respect. When Mercury and Uranus are combined, gales from the northwest pile up snow in tremendous drifts during cold seasons. These storms tie up traffic and communications.

Radio reception has been observed to improve under major stations of Uranus, for static electricity in the atmosphere then appears to reach a minimum. An exception, as we referred to previously under interpretations of Jupiter, are the negative angles formed between Jupiter and Uranus, including the conjunction.

A leading newspaper columnist (New York Sun, April 10, 1939) stated that atop Mt. Washington, 6,293 feet high, in New Hampshire, on April 12, 1934 there was clocked the highest wind velocity ever recorded by man, 231 miles per hour. Some explorers, however have insisted that much greater wind velocities have been observed though not officially recorded in the interior of Asia. This is quite probable since Mt. Everest, in the Himalayas, is exactly five and a half miles (29,902 feet) high—the loftiest in the world—and nearly five times the height of Mt. Washington. Wind velocity increases with altitude and probably will be one of the major problems for solution when aviation flights in the stratosphere become general. Greatest difficulty may be experienced bucking terrific head winds during westward flights in the stratosphere when Uranus influences are operating. Altitude appears to affect temperatures and wind velocity similarly as geographic latitude, the highest altitudes being equivalent to highest latitudes.

6.03—URANUS WITH SUN:

Under any configuration, or when in parallel of declination, the Sun with Uranus increases negative electricity in the atmosphere, induces high barometric pressure, appreciable and sudden decline of temperature with accompanying increasing wind velocity that may range from fresh northwest winds to erratic gales. The key word of Uranus is gusty since winds under the influence of this planet are seldom, if ever, steady. Lowest temperatures, under this influence, will be observed in those geographical areas where Uranus occupied the lower meridian at the Sun's ingress during the previous quarter. High pressure areas thereat will veer northward to higher altitudes and push cold masses of air south and downslope. Where Uranus occupies the south angle at seasonal quarters, high pressure areas will veer southward where comparatively colder weather will be experienced than over the interior. Also note points 90 degrees from these meridians as originating points of the Uranus conditions and time them eastward from such points of observation at the rate of approximately 12 degrees of geographical longitude daily, noting particularly when the Moon conjoins or opposes the lower meridian of the solar quarter chart at points of observation eastward. This marks the path of local distribution of atmospheric conditions picked up from points of origin or key points westward. Herein may be found one of the primary keys to long range weather prognosis.

The Sun-Uranus configurations usually produce atmospheric changes close to time of their culmination but their greatest intensity may not reach your place of observation until a few days later during colder seasons. In summer, however, under any aspects, storms may develop near mountains or highlands as cold currents sweep downward to the valleys and lowlands generally. The conjunction, opposition, square and semi-square (including the parallel) are conducive to disturbing, chilly and gusty weather. Changes are sudden. The Sun conjunction Uranus is formed approximately four to five days later each year. When these configurations take place in the summer season, bathing resorts feel the results. During the first week of May, 1942, following Sun conjunction both Saturn and Uranus, there will be ample opportunity for skeptical minds to test out relations between planetary phenomena and atmospheric changes.

6.04—URANUS WITH NEPTUNE:

Uranus applies to the slower moving Neptune and to Pluto, though as yet we know little or nothing weatherwise concerning effects of the latter. Configurations of Uranus and Neptune are rare as compared with those between other heavenly bodies. The last conjunction of those major planets took place during February, 1821, in Capricorn 2.00. On January 31, 1907 Uranus, in Capricorn 10.27, formed an opposition to Neptune in Cancer 10.27. The next quadrature aspect between these bodies does not take place until the fall of 1953, when Uranus, in Cancer 23, will square Neptune in Libra 23.00.

Configurations between those major planets are rare, but the effects on weather are enduring and similar in character to those of Venus and Uranus. Precipitation should be above the normal average, with extremes of temperatures, frequent fogs in the lowlands and generally freak weather throughout the world.

In checking over the planetary positions at the time of the earthquake and destructive fire that devastated San Francisco on April 18, 1906, 5:12:06 a.m. Standard Time, it is interesting to note that Uranus, retrograde and tenanting Capricorn 8° 29', opposed Neptune in Cancer 7° 52'. Mercury was then applying to square aspects with both Uranus and Neptune. Mars was exactly semi-square Neptune and forming a 135 degree angle with Uranus. It is very likely that the opposition of Uranus and Neptune intensified the San Francisco earthquake.

6.05—STATISTICAL DATA: URANUS:

(a) Uranus in the Equator: According to Pearce's Textbook, Part II, p. 164, Uranus was in the equator May 29, 1843, March 11, 1844, November 14, 1884 and February 28, 1885. On each occasion, either gales and squally rain or very cold weather accompanied these stations. On February 24, 1928, Uranus occupied Aries 1° 46' and received a sextile aspect from Venus in 1° 46' of the crystallizing sign Aquarius. On February 25, the temperature dropped suddenly to 20 degrees below zero at Saranac Lake, N.Y., the cold wave reaching New York City that evening culminating in a minimum temperature of 6 degrees. (Refer to 6.02).

(b) <u>Uranus squared by Saturn</u>: In the map for the Summer Solstice, June 22, 1931, 75th meridian, 4:28 a.m., Pisces 4.00 occupied the Midheaven and Uranus, tenanting Aries 18.55, was on the upper meridian at Long. 31 West, squared by Saturn in Capricorn 21.28R, hence indicating abnormal weather over southern areas from Long. 31 W. and eastward to Europe. On July 21 Saturn formed the exact square to Uranus from Capricorn 19° 22'. On July 26, Uranus attained a stationary position in Aries 19° 23'. Since Uranus occupied the <u>south</u> angle of the solstice chart at Long. 31 W., the <u>southern areas</u> responded to the maximum effects.

In the New York <u>Herald Tribune</u> dated September 6, 1931, under the caption "Wettest, Most Sunless and Coldest August since 1900 Breaks Three Records", we read the following item:

"PARIS, FRANCE—Sept.3, 1931—Summer is over and yet France has scarcely seen any summer this year. The sun came out in June for the races of the Grande Semaine, but it disappeared on July 3 and tourists who came to France to enjoy the summer months have not seen it since. August has beaten in fact three records for bad weather; it has been the <u>wettest</u>, most <u>sunless</u> and <u>coldest</u> August since the century's beginning. There have been days when the temperature fell to 44 degrees. The <u>total</u> number of sunny hours has not exceeded 100, whereas the most sunless previous August, in 1912, gave 120 hours of sunshine." (refer to 5.03)

(c) <u>Uranus on the Lower Meridian</u>: The ingress map for September 23, 1930, 1:36 p.m., 75th meridian, showed Libra 27 on the midheaven and Capricorn 2° 52' on the ascendant. Uranus, in Aries 13° 56', retrograde, occupied the lower meridian at Long. 89° W. On October 19, Mercury, by transit, came to the opposition of this point and a record cold wave from the Canadian Rockies veered south and eastward across the Middle West, then traced northward into Northern New York and New England. Sub-zero temperatures were reported from North Dakota. A <u>blizzard</u> (in October!) with a four foot depth of snow, covered to area from Erie, Pa. to Buffalo,

forcing hundreds to quit autos on highways leading to Buffalo. Traffic
was disrupted generally. On October 20 a minimum temperature of
36 degrees was reported at New York City and a fifty-mile-an-hour
northwest gale swept the New Jersey coast. Snowfall continued
heavy over Buffalo, N. Y. and adjacent areas. (Refer to 1.07 and
6.02).

(d) <u>Uranus Stationary</u>: At the Sun's ingress into Capricorn on
December 22, 1930, 8:40 a.m. 75th meridian time, the Midheaven
yielded Scorpio 12 and the Ascendant was Capricorn 12° 23'. Uranus
was stationary in Aries 11° 27' and was on the nadir at Long. 106°
W. On January 6, 1931, Great Salt Lake, one of the saltiest bodies
of water in the world, succumbed to the cold in that geographical
area. Ice was found on the lake for the first time in the history of
the weather bureau. A. B. Burton, Geological Survey engineer,
reported that he found ice a quarter of an inch thick beginning at
the shore and extending out 1,000 feet. The lake water is
approximately 23 per cent salt.*

(e) <u>URANUS squared by Jupiter</u>: On January 18, 1938, Uranus
was stationary in Taurus 9° 43'. Jupiter, in Aquarius 6° 29', was
applying to a square aspect which culminated on January 31. Wire
communications throughout Canada were disrupted on January
17 by interference attributed to the manifestations of the Aurora
Borealis. On the 18th, temperatures at zero were recorded in New
York City, 16 below at Albany, N.Y. and 42 below from points in the
Province of Quebec. On January 26, brilliant manifestations of the
Northern Lights were reported all over Europe as far south as
Gibraltar. On January 29, a 90-mile-an-hour gale, with
accompanying rain and sleet, raked the British Isles. (Refer to 4.04).

(f) <u>Uranus conjoined by Jupiter</u>: On January 25, 1928, Jupiter
and Uranus formed a conjunction in Aries 0° 26'. Mercury formed a
semi-square to both bodies on that day from Aquarius 15° 26'.
Although official records of the local weather bureau at New York
City for that date reported a maximum wind velocity of 70 miles per
hour at New York on January 25, it was estimated that in some
parts of the metropolitan area the wind reached a velocity of 90
miles an hour. Store windows were blown in and shattered in all
parts of the city, particularly along the waterfronts. Numerous

*<u>Note under (d)</u>: At the Winter Solstice, Dec. 22, 1930, 8:40 a.m. 75th meridian,
Uranus was stationary over the 106th meridian, squared by Saturn in the ascendant.
On January 2 following, the Sun squared Uranus. On January 5 the Sun was
conjoined with Saturn and on the 6th was conjunction with Mercury. The Moon
was in perigee on January 6th.

persons were injured by falling signs and other objects blown from aloft in business sections of the city.

(g) <u>Uranus on lower meridian at Solstice</u>: <u>New England hurricane, Sept 21,1938</u>

The devastating tropical hurricane which battered the coast from Long Island to Cape Cod on September 21, 1938 resulted in a reported toll of 491 dead, 60,000 homeless and property damage from winds, floods and tidal waves estimated at half a billion dollars. The tropical storm was first reported on Sept. 18 north of Puerto Rico. It moved west toward the Bahamas and on Sept. 20, 8:30 p.m. D.S.T. was east of Florida, due south of Cape Hatteras. The disturbance then veered straight north passing east of Cape Hatteras on the 21 at 8:30 a.m. and reaching Westhampton, Long Island on the 21 at 3:30 p.m. Winds in the New York and New Jersey coast areas were so strong that trees were blown into houses.

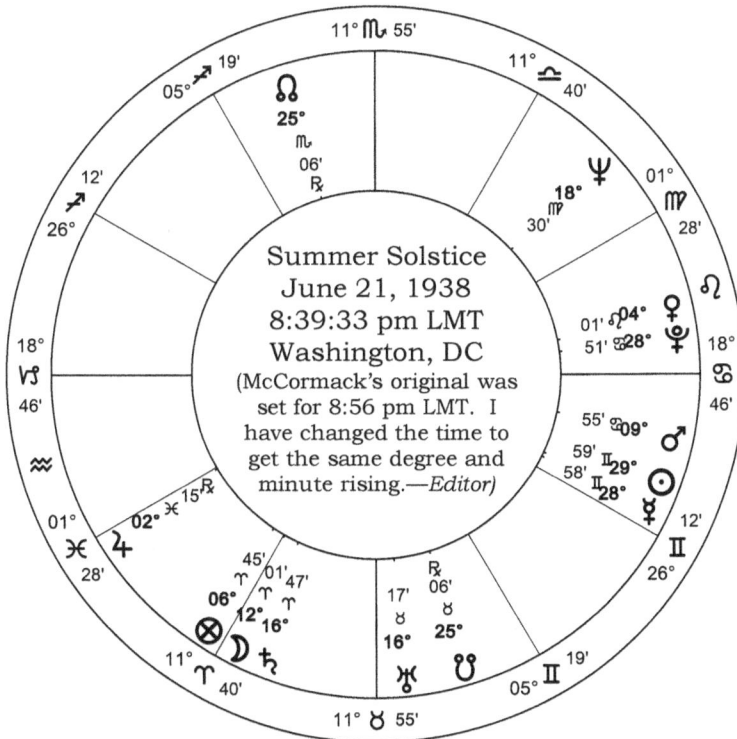

Summer Solstice
June 21, 1938
8:39:33 pm LMT
Washington, DC
(McCormack's original was set for 8:56 pm LMT. I have changed the time to get the same degree and minute rising.—Editor)

The disturbance pursued a course through the Connecticut River valley, demolishing woodlands and property. Following the excessive downpour, the Connecticut River at Hartford, Conn. on September

23 reached the crest of a 35.11 feet flood.

We have repeatedly directed attention to solar eclipses as related to events affecting masses of people at one time rather than individuals. In Astrotech, May 27, 1938, p. 479, in commenting on the chart for the solar eclipse of May 29, 1938, in Gemini 7° 32', we specifically referred to the transit of Mars (Virgo 7° 32') squaring this point on September 19 as a point of disturbance. It is also pertinent to mention here that where Uranus occupies the nadir in a solstice or equinoctial chart, property damage hazards are always greatest. In the chart here illustrated, Uranus occupied the lower meridian at Long. 73° W. and the tropical hurricane entered the mainland exactly at this geographic locale (Westhampton, Long Island).

7

EFFECTS OF THE PLANET NEPTUNE
ON THE WEATHER

7.01—GENERAL:

NEPTUNE, which is astrologically considered as the higher octave of the planet Venus, was discovered by Galle, of Berlin, on September 23, 1846, as the result of calculations by LeVerrier. This stellar body has a diameter of over 36,500 miles, is over 2,746,271,000 miles distant from the Sun and completes its orbital revolution in 164.788 years. The equinoctial and tropical stations of this planet are, therefore, rare.

The keynotes of Neptune's influence weatherwise are variability, low visibility, ascending air currents, prevalent southerly winds, lower barometer, humidity, excessive static and vacuums in the higher air strata that often prove hazardous for aviation. In cool seasons induces fogs; in summer, sudden changes varying from dead calms to squalls and destructive cyclones within narrow geographical areas. Impressions are sudden in proportion to higher ranges of temperature. Dead calms with attendant excessive humidity and rapidly declining barometer are potential danger signals.

As the extreme expression of the Venus influence, this planet induces the heaviest downpours in the shortest space of time. During spells of heat, combined with excessive humidity under Neptune's influence, surface air currents ascend vertically, carrying dust particles in large quantities into the upper atmosphere. Disturbances in the upper air levels are sometimes generated so quickly that a spiral motion is set in operation, forming like an inverted cone. These cloud formations have the effect of vacuums. As these lowering dark clouds sweep in from the western horizon, preceded by increasing wind velocity, the intense atmospheric turbulences sweep along narrow paths not more than a mile wide across country. Such storms are intensified in the lowlands and along waterways, when attended by preceding high temperature.

75

The temperature invariably rises under the Neptune influence. Even in the midst of winter, humid, calm atmospheric conditions first develop <u>mild</u> weather, resulting in heavy fogs, particularly at night. Because Neptune disturbances are confined to such narrow limits and seldom continue in a direct line but rather follow the lowlands, it is more prudent to judge generally than to interpret specific forecasts for a local place. Frequently, while the south wind is operating, the squalls will build up around <u>sandy</u> soil in the warm months, especially along the seashore or waterways. The lows sometimes build up in the north and follow waterways southward, picking up in intensity as they wend their way to the coast and lowlands. Action will frequently depend on the character of other planets configurated therewith. In any case, expect <u>sudden changes</u>, threatening weather. In warmer seasons, under adverse aspects from Mars, Sun or Mercury, small sailing craft on open waters may encounter sudden squalls. The official weather forecasters issue coastal storm warnings. Increasing haze, accompanied by a peculiar calm are signals of this approaching phenomenon. In hot summer the severest sunburns are experienced during these Neptune aspects.

In winter and cold seasons, smoke fogs develop over the larger cities. Sunlight is at a minimum, but temperatures are mild. The atmosphere is "sticky." When Neptune occupies the lower meridian at the December or March solar ingresses, sudden thaws threaten flood hazards. Many years of practical observations lead us to the conclusion that the planet Neptune is indicative of excessive moisture. When Venus adds its influence, the downfall is abnormal and heaviest downpours occur in the shortest period of time. It is a most peculiar phenomenon that Venus conjunction Neptune downpours are accompanied by a perfect calm—absolutely no wind.

Neptune conjoined, opposed or squared by Jupiter, Saturn or Uranus inclines to epidemic diseases arising from extremes of weather. Probably is related to <u>contagion</u>.

7.02—<u>MAJOR STATIONS OF NEPTUNE</u>:
Since the planet Neptune attains extreme declination or crosses the equator at periods of approximately 41 years, the chief positions for more frequent observations are when occupying the meridian (particularly the lower meridian) of the seasonal ingress charts or in lunation maps, when in square to the meridian, when apparently stationary in longitude, or when in conjunction, parallel of declination, opposed by or squared by the Sun. All these stations or configurations incline to lowering barometer which may be rapid

in mild seasons. Excessive humidity and precipitation, with stagnant atmosphere which is so frequently referred to as "sticky" and enervating. In summer, peculiar calms followed by squally storms. In cooler seasons, expect fogs, particularly at night.

The Sun's sextile, trine and minor 30 and 150 degree aspects are conducive to fair and mild weather with breezy atmosphere, favorable for sailing craft. Nevertheless, when Neptune is concerned it is advisable to carefully weigh all attendant planetary phenomena. We suggest noting in preceding lectures the effects of other planets when in positive or negative aspects with Neptune, including the conjunctions. When the slow moving planets Jupiter, Saturn or Uranus are in conjunction or adverse aspects with Neptune, weather may be greatly disturbed throughout the world intermittently for months at a time.

Neptune was in the equator May 15 and August 22, 1862 and again on March 15, November 25 and November 28, 1863. On January 3, 1942, attaining a stationary position in Virgo 29° 53' and again stationary in Libra 2° 04' on January 5, 1943, these major stations so close to the equator will afford ample opportunity to study the planet's influence on weather. On November 1, 1943, Neptune will occupy Libra 3° 05' with 0° 00' declination, thus marking its actual transit over the equator. Venus conjunction Neptune in Libra 3° 28' and both in the equator on November 13, 1943, should provide a good opportunity to study the influence of this planetary combination for inducing excessive downfall within a short period of time. On July 2, 1944 Saturn, occupying the North Tropic in Cancer 1° 34', will form an exact quadrature to Neptune in the equator (Libra 1° 34'), thus tending to upset weather conditions throughout the northern hemisphere due to excessive atmospheric depressions, abnormal moisture and threats of floods where either Saturn or Neptune occupy the meridian at the preceding Summer Solstice.

January, 1945 indicates a period of unusually foggy weather with attendant anomalies of weather. On January 10, immediately following Neptune's stationary position in the equator (Libra 6.26), Saturn will again square this planet from Cancer 6.26 in the North Tropic. Immediately following the preceding Winter Solstice in December (1944), when the Sun opposes Saturn and squares the degree held by Neptune the combined influences of these major bodies will be generated in the atmosphere. For detailed interpretation refer to 5.04.

North Tropic: Neptune attained extreme north declination (22 N 23) or North Tropic station during May, 1903, the Sun forming a conjunction with Neptune in that position on June 26, 1903, at New Moon.

Neptune on the Meridian in Seasonal Ingress Charts:

The immortal A. J. Pearce, in his Textbook of Astrology which is replete with valuable astro-meteorological instructions and statistical data, records the fact that at the Summer Solstice of 1879 the planet Neptune tenanted the lower meridian at Greenwich. The Sun (in sextile aspect to Uranus) and Mercury were setting in the chart. A cold and wet summer was disastrous for agriculturists in the British Isles. At the Royal Observatory, rainfall in July, 1879 was 3.72 inches, 1.35 inches greater than the average for the previous 38 years. That August the rainfall was 5.19 inches, being 2.77 inches greater than the average. We quote this record to compare with subsequently observed characteristics evidenced in weather when Neptune occupied a similar angle in ingress charts over the United States.

Our own observations concerning Neptune on the meridian of the solar charts for the beginning of the seasons lead us to believe that 10th house (south angle) positions are equally important as provocative of veering lower barometric pressure areas and static conditions southward, with accompanying excessive condensation of aqueous vapors in the lowlands and colder, wet weather over the interior as winds blow downslope toward the centers of atmospheric disturbance.

The nadir or 4th house position, on the other hand, induces low pressure areas to veer northward. Fed by winds from the southward, the resultant ascending air currents work upslope to the interior. Deluges, developing in the northern areas, swell the streams and increase the flood hazards in the lowlands. When interpreting the meridian position of Neptune, it is important, therefore, to observe whether the planet occupies the lower or upper meridian. Likewise note those longitudes where Neptune exactly squares the meridian for in each case these points are critical for excessive downfall or abnormally wet seasons.

Should Venus transit the place of Neptune, or oppose it while thus stationed, the tendency to induce excessive downfall of rain within a short space of time at such configurations is accentuated. In most cases the effects of Neptune are extreme. Rapid fall of barometer, accompanied by heavy mist and calm atmosphere are approaching signals of such phenomena.

7.03—STATISTICAL DATA: NEPTUNE

(a) Neptune on the Meridian: During 1927, in pursuing research studies of chart indications and actual weather conditions, we maintained a daily record in typed form together with other statistical data recorded during that period and which we have on record in our files. These records fully attest to the 4th house influence of Neptune for high average of downfall.

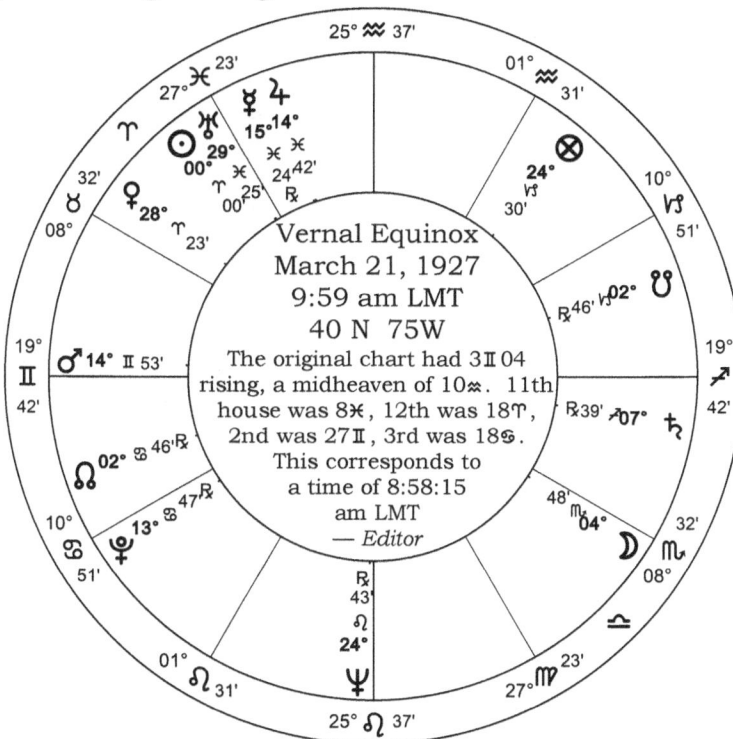

Vernal Equinox
March 21, 1927
9:59 am LMT
40 N 75W
The original chart had 3Ⅱ04 rising, a midheaven of 10☓. 11th house was 8✶, 12th was 18♈, 2nd was 27Ⅱ, 3rd was 18♋.
This corresponds to a time of 8:58:15 am LMT
— Editor

The accompanying map for the Vernal Ingress on March 21, 1927, 9:59 a.m., 75th meridian, as copied from our record, shows Neptune in the 4th angle. During the spring season of that year the rainfall was considerably above the average in the Ohio valley and over the Eastern States generally. Uranus, entering the equator, was upsetting normal weather conditions all over the world, particularly in Europe where it occupied the upper meridian. According to newspaper reports on April 24, 1927, the Mississippi River was overflowing its banks and spreading desolation. Appeals for relief were sent out by the inhabitants along the lower Mississippi when their homes were washed away by the flood.

(b) A map of the heavens for the Sun's ingress into Capricorn on December 21, 1936, 5:18 p.m. 107th meridian embodies some interesting features relative to the Neptune influence since this chart was practically applied in a test forecast for a newspaper. At that longitude Neptune, occupying the lower meridian, was being opposed by Saturn from the upper meridian, the actual opposition having taken place on January 17, 1937. On January 22-23 Venus formed a conjunction with Saturn and opposed Neptune. Based on these testimonies, interpretations, prepared in December, 1936, were submitted in writing to a syndicated newspaper columnist as a conservative test of the principles involved.* It was definitely stated that these combinations indicated hazards for aviation over that geographical area as the result of ice forming on wings of airplanes in transit. This forecast was confirmed by the large number of airplane disasters. Official investigations disclosed that invariably the crashes resulted from ice rapidly forming on the wings.

Winter Solstice
December 21 1936
5:18 pm LMT
40 N   107 W

(*Neal O'Hara, New York <u>Post</u>, subsequently printed verification of forecasts.)

The winter season was colder and more inclement over the western portions of the United States. Over the Middle West and Eastern States, on the contrary, comparatively milder temperatures and lower average of precipitation were attested by Mars in the north angle of the chart. The midway point between Neptune and Mars measured geographically to the longitude of Chicago. Therefore, on January 25, 1937, devastating floods swept down the Ohio and Mississippi valleys and on January 29 the reported toll was 330 persons dead (225 of them in Kentucky). In ten different States from Pennsylvania to Mississippi, 1,035,000 persons were rendered homeless.

The accompanying map illustrates the relative positions of the heavenly bodies at the Winter Solstice, December 21, 1936, 5:18 p.m., Local Mean Time, 107° West Long.

It should be borne in mind that these maps, for either solar quarters from which to interpret seasonal indications or weekly lunar quarters from which to discern weekly changes in the character of the weather, may be erected for the longitude and latitude of the place in which you reside.

They may also be transposed to any desired point in geographical longitude by deducting four minutes of time for each degree west and adding in the same manner for meridians eastward from any given point.

(c) In the map for the Winter Solstice of December 22, 1937, 1:14 A.M., Washington, D.C., (6:22 am Greenwich Mean Time) the midheaven was Cancer 18⁰ and the Ascendant was Libra 15.43. Neptune occupied Virgo 21° 09'. After a year, during the same seasonal quarter, we find Neptune on the lower meridian at a point approximately 87° westward and occupying the meridian at approximately 166° East Long. where heaviest precipitation would be expected to materialize and require eight to nine days for the weather movement to continue eastward to the Atlantic Seaboard. Such movements would change in character in transit according to related positions of heavenly bodies with the meridian at the respective points of observation. The Moon to the upper or lower meridian or in square thereto at any meridian in terms of the solar key charts usually marks the times of those important changes in weather. During the Winter season here discussed, Venus was on the lower meridian at 108° West longitude and in square to Neptune, hence indicating a geographic locale where the precipitation would be excessive and with <u>Venus</u> increasing the tendencies to <u>snow</u>.

(d) <u>Seismic and volcanic Phenomena</u>:

The frequency of volcanic eruptions and seismic disturbances coinciding with outbreaks of pestilential diseases tends to support the hypothesis of planetary action being the exciting cause of all these phenomena. And electricity may be the agent. For instance, in astro-meteorological forecasts for 1926 prepared for and published in the Brooklyn <u>Daily Citizen</u>, November 15, 1925, we pointed out that unusual seismic and volcanic disturbances during the year would be followed by pandemic diseases in various parts of the world. During 1926, Vesuvius became unusually violent. Volcanic eruptions in the Pacific Ocean and in the Far East were recorded. Epidemics of disease broke out over restricted areas during the summer of 1926 when the planet Mars, attaining its <u>perihelion</u> station, was a contributing factor. Typhus in epidemic form was reported from China and Italy on August 20. Jupiter was then applying to a quadrature of the planet Saturn after separating from an opposition with <u>Neptune</u>, Jupiter being tenanted in <u>Scorpio</u>, which sign is related to <u>eruptions</u>.

Observations over a number of years lead us to believe that configurations from the sign Scorpio, particularly when Jupiter and other major planets are concerned, are conducive to volcanic eruptions. Sepharial (W. Gorn Old) after considerable investigation, expressed the opinion that Mars either in conjunction or opposition to Neptune was a powerful combination for exciting seismic phenomena and that the position of Saturn on the meridian indicates the locality where effects may be maximum.

There is a close relationship between meteorology and seismology, since both weather changes and seismic phenomena are related to planetary action. Observation and statistics indicate that earthquakes follow solar eclipses also, when the point of eclipse is "sparked" by transits of major planets. This subject will be discussed in detail later.

8

OTHER FACTORS NECESSARY
FOR DETAILED FORECASTS

8.01—<u>GENERAL</u>:

In venturing prognoses of the weather either for seasons or for minor periods, the following essentials should be duly considered: (1) The general character of the geographic area, weatherwise, as the results of latitude and altitude. (2) The solar ingress for the season at the point of observation under inquiry should be used for major reference and all interpretations for minor periods also referred to this map. Note carefully whether any major planets occupy the nadir or the upper meridian either at or immediately westward of the place of observation, For example, planets in the 3rd house will be affecting weather in the north. If Taurus 0 degrees should be on the lower meridian and Uranus is tenanted in Taurus 15 degrees, the effects will be most potent and frequent during the period about 15 degrees westward in longitude and over the northern areas. If occupying the same distance from the midheaven and occupying the 9th house, the effects would be felt in the same distance to the westward but more generally over the southern areas, because Uranus occupies the south angle. Similarly, note those days when the Moon, Sun or other significators form conjunctions, oppositions or squares to planets thus stationed, since these configurations usually time important changes of weather in accordance with the combined natures of the significators. (3) The geology of areas under inquiry also deserves careful consideration, particularly during the warmer seasons when local atmospheric disturbances develop more frequently than in the cooler seasons. New York City, surrounded by water, is more responsive to humidity. The Pennsylvania coal fields would attract the full affect of the Saturn rays and the position of Saturn at the Vernal Equinox, March 21, 1938, 1;43 A.M., 75th meridian, when Aries 25 occupies the lower meridian, should be interesting for observation in this respect. (4) Consider the Sun as the day marker, noting carefully those days when it forms strong aspects with or conjoins the significators. The Moon is generally considered the hour hand and when joining with the Sun in aspects, particularly when the Moon is in perigee, in the equator or in the north tropic it contributes largely towards exciting the influence of the planets in the atmosphere. The Moon is also an important time marker in tracing the course of certain weather conditions from a point of origin and eastward round the globe. When the Moon transits the lower meridian of the last solar ingress the type of weather indicated by such position will veer northward. If transiting the midheaven, the high or low barometric pressure condition will veer southward. This brings us to the subject of storm tracks as applicable to the United States.

8.02—STORM TRACKS:

If a low pressure area does not originate in the United States, it enters it from the northwest, west, or south. Those which enter north of the middle of the country have a tendency, in crossing the Mississippi Valley, to move towards the south and then recurve towards the northeast. In approaching the Atlantic Coast, all lows move towards the northeast. Although low pressure areas may originate within the country or enter it from various directions, they nearly always leave it by way of the St. Lawrence Valley and Newfoundland. The average velocity for all tracks for all times of the year is 31.7 miles per hour. The winter velocity is, however, nearly twice as large as summer—(January, 40; June and July, 24.9). It is also a very important fact that the number of lows in winter is more than double the number in summer. Nevertheless, localized perturbances over limited areas in summer seasons are sometimes extremely puzzling to conventional weather forecasters. A low, or storm area, nevertheless, may loiter for a day or two, drifting, perhaps, but one or two hundred miles in that time. Another low may rush across the country, covering a distance of sixteen or seventeen hundred miles in a single day.

                                                                    3-12-38

8.03—SEASONAL INDICATIONS:

The general character of the weather for a season over any required point of observation is inferred from charts of the solar ingresses. Although configurations or primary positions of the significators indicate the time of various weather changes, we must revert to the ingress charts to determine the geographic locale where these conditions originate or their effects are most potent. Points where planets are directly on the meridian or in angles of 90 degrees or 45 degrees thereto should be noted. The nature of the sign on the cusp of the 4th house should also be duly considered. Conjunctions, parallels of declination, oppositions, squares and sextile aspects of the Sun with other bodies should be carefully noted as these configurations induce important weather changes which then pursue an eastward direction around the globe. Planets in the 3rd and 9th houses influence weather immediately westward of the point of observation which is later affected by their movement in an easterly direction.

In order to get a clearer picture of relative positions of planets to the meridian over different parts of the country, begin with the chart below for the Vernal Equinox, March 21, 1938, 1:43 A.M. at the 75th meridian. The longitudes of the planets will remain the same in all charts but the midheaven and other house positions will change as charts are transposed for geographic points east or west of the observation point. Erect similar charts for other meridians westward as follows:

March 21	0:43 am	Long. 90 W.	MC Libra	10
March 20	11:43 pm	Long. 105 W.	MC Virgo	22.30
March 20	10:43 pm	Long. 120 W.	MC Virgo	06.00

Count East ← | → Count West

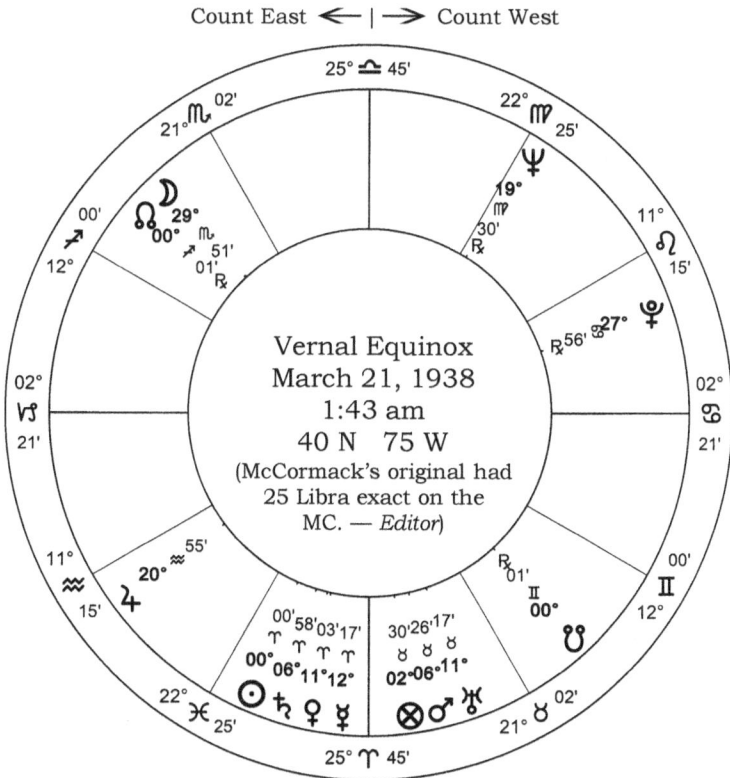

Vernal Equinox
March 21, 1938
1:43 am
40 N   75 W
(McCormack's original had
25 Libra exact on the
MC. — Editor)

After some experience with these maps you can simplify procedure by working from one key map from the geographic area of observation. For instance, in order to ascertain the meridian where Neptune will occupy the midheaven we count the number of degrees from the midheaven at 75 degrees west. This amounts to 35½ degrees which we add to 75.00 W and accordingly interpret that Neptune will occupy the upper meridian and affect southern areas at Long. 110.30 W. Counting eastward, these differences in longitude are deducted. Therefore, in deducting the distance of 16 degrees, the distance of Uranus from the lower meridian, we note that Uranus will occupy the lower meridian at Long. 59.00 W.

8:04—MOON AS IMPORTANT TIME MARKER:

The Moon, which operates as an important time marker as distributor of moisture, has a daily motion of approximately 12 degrees and makes a circuit of the chart in 28 days. Sometimes its movement is accelerated and at other times slow. Note those days when the Moon transits the upper or lower meridian or square of these points, for then it brings to culmination the weather conditions generated at points westward. In lesser degree, the semi-square aspects to the meridian are effective. These angles explain the seven and three-and-a half day cycles of low or high pressure areas that sometimes accompany major planetary conditions. The Moon merely traces the course of and times weather changes already indicated by planetary positions or combinations in the charts. Transiting the fourth house, the Moon inclines the high or low pressure areas northward. Passing over the midheaven, it veers their paths over southerly courses. The radical positions of planets in the ingress chart afford index to the general character of these periodical weather changes, as will also transits affecting those points. In this respect, the Moon sometimes sets into operation the combined characters of two planets approaching a conjunction some days ahead of the actual culmination of such configuration.

8.05—TIDES IN THE AIR:

In a syndicated series entitled "Strange As It Seems," by John Hix, dated February 22, 1938, we read:

"Strange as it seems, the atmosphere rises and falls in daily tides just as the ocean does. As a matter of fact, even the ground we walk on is subject to the pulsing, gravitational swells brought about by the attraction of the Moon.

"The air tides possess many features in common with ocean

tides, according to scientists. One is a small oscillatory variation in the atmospheric pressure, they claim, regarded as a superposition of harmonic constituents with the ordinary tidal periods."

With reference to the foregoing, exhaustive astro-meteorological investigations indicate that all the planetary bodies, particularly the major planets, exert gravitational pulls on the earth (1) when occupying certain magnetic angles in relation to the meridian at the place on observation on the earth, (2) when affecting by transit in conjunction with or in aspect to the degree in which a recent solar eclipse took place, especially when the planet Mars is the exciting factor, (3) when major planets occupy certain positions in their orbits. For example, the triple combination of Jupiter-Saturn and Uranus in the earth sign Taurus during the spring of 1941 indicates an enormous tidal pull that may result in the most severe seismic disturbances in eighty years. It has also been indicated by statistical data that there is a connection between the fluctuations of the annual death rate and the position of Jupiter in its orbit.

Based on our own investigations over a period of many years, it is our opinion that both the planets Jupiter and Mars influence certain types of seismic phenomena resulting from expansion within the earth's interior. Saturn affects through contraction. Uranus is more spasmodic and erratic. There appears to be a tidal action on the liquid lava in the interior of the earth which may have a certain connection with the production of earthquakes and volcanic activity. In this respect the planet Neptune may be closely related.

Seismic shocks are greater in number when the Moon is in perigee (nearest the earth) than when in apogee (farthest from the earth). In the daily rotation of the earth, shocks occur most frequently when the Moon is near the meridian or on the horizon and these observations, substantiated by statistical data, were submitted by Alfred J. Pearce, in his <u>Textbook of Astrology</u>, p. 207, as early as 1885. Some of our present day scientists are therefore only now "discovering" scientific facts that have been a matter of printed record for more than eighty years, if not longer.

8.06—PERIGEE, AND PERIHELION POSITIONS:
It should be borne in mind that when a planet is in perigee (nearest the earth) or perihelion (nearest to the Sun), or stationary, it acts with much greater force than at other times; consequently when two or more planets are in line with the earth and one is in perigee, the resultant planetary attraction is great, and accordingly,

the rainfall and disturbance of the atmosphere are increased proportionally. In view of the importance of the perigee and perihelion positions of the major planets, it seems desirable that astronomical ephemerides include the time of such phenomena in annual issues for purposes of research study.

8.07—ELECTRIC SIGNS OF THE ZODIAC: Aries, Gemini, Leo, Libra, Sagittarius and Aquarius.

8.08—ELECTRIC PLANETS: Sun, Mars, Jupiter, Mercury and Uranus.

8.09—MAJOR CONJUNCTIONS:
    When major planets form conjunctions, consider chiefly the places in geographic longitude where they are situated on the lower meridian, or where they are southing, rising or setting at the moment of the phenomenon. 3-26-'38

8.10—HIGH AND LOW PRESSURE AREAS EXPLAINED:
    A high pressure area is a section where the atmospheric pressure is heavy, or what is the same thing, the barometer is high. An aneroid barometer, on which the graduations of pressure are indicated by an index hand in hundredths of an inch serves a useful purpose in noting changes of atmospheric pressure, especially during warm months when localized changes are likely to occur rather suddenly. A high pressure area is the region of descending air and usually clear, pleasant weather with a tendency to cooler temperatures may be expected in the vicinity as air currents sweep downslope if the high pressure area veers northward of the point of observation. If, however, the high pressure area should pass a point to the southward of the observation point, it will tend to blow winds from the warmer southern latitudes northward, with accompanying elevation of temperature. Abnormal high pressure areas under signatures of Uranus, particularly when situated in the 4th house of an ingress or lunar quarter chart inclines these high pressure areas to the northerly lanes, with resulting temperatures below the normal for the period. Wind velocities from descending vertical air currents are then accentuated. Such a general condition will be indicated for the North Atlantic States during the Summer of 1938, more particularly over the New England States. The primary cause of this is shown by the nadir position of Uranus in the chart below.

Summer Solstice
June 21, 1938
8:56 pm T.L.T.
(8:39:33 pm L.M.T.)
Washington, DC

This is a most instructive map because it will serve to explain the wide differentials of temperature between the meridian of Denver, Col. when low pressure areas will indicate more frequent development over northerly areas and the North Atlantic States where prevailing colder temperatures increase downfall as these low pressure areas advance eastward.

A <u>low</u> pressure area or region of low barometer is that of <u>ascending</u> air currents frequently preceded by warmer temperatures and bad weather may be expected in its vicinity. High pressure areas are often spoken of as the anti-storm, and low pressure as the storm area. It is suggested that these high and low pressure areas be studied from day to day during cooler seasons and that their paths be traced on the official weather bureau maps as an aid to short range weather prognosis and in checking against astrographic indications. In the above chart, Saturn occupies the nadir at 103 degrees west longitude and emphasizes the low pressure areas in that locale. The result impairs crops due to lows veering northward and resulting excessive rainfall in the south, following spells of excessive heat as winds sweep from the south. The time factors will be when the Moon forms a conjunction, square or opposition to Saturn.   Intense storm periods may be expected when the Sun squares Saturn in that geographical area on July 10, even while temperatures simultaneously fall suddenly over the North Atlantic States. Another period of intense atmospheric disturbance over the Mississippi Valley is indicated over July 31-August 1 as Saturn attains a stationary position and is opposed by the Moon near the equator.

While Federal meteorologists are expected to explain the peculiar abnormalities of wet and cool weather in the United States, Mars' north tropic position will be receiving greatest emphasis over Europe where its nadir position will be indicative of burning heat, particularly on and immediately after July 24th when the Sun forms a conjunction therewith in the calorific sign Leo.   Again, scientists will be erroneously ascribing all these peculiar weather conditions to sunspot activity.   In giving not only primary planetary causes of such phenomena but also indicating specific dates two to three months in advance and dated, these observations can best speak for themselves.   4-18-'38

9

EPIDEMIC DISEASE AND WEATHER

9.01—PLANETARY CAUSES IGNORED:

From remotest antiquity the causes of atmospheric phenomena have been sought among the phenomena of the heavens. In our opinion based upon years of exhaustive researches, we are convinced that to abandon this research is to render the discovery of the laws which regulate the weather, hopeless. The Federal meteorologists, by plotting daily weather maps and depending upon mechanical devices for determining barometric pressure, temperatures, direction and velocity of winds, etc., can venture fairly reliable predictions of the weather 24 hours in advance, except during the extreme warm periods; but beyond that they are dealing with uncertainties and confining weather prognoses mostly to prudent guesses. A careful check-up of their daily forecasts during July and August of any year will confirm this statement.

9.02—ASSEMBLING SCIENTIFIC DATA:

We must watch for coincidences between astronomic and atmospheric phenomena, referring to ingress and lunation charts as index keys to places where planets happen to be in magnetic line or angle to certain meridians on the earth. As a learned astro-meteorologist once observed: "Watching for coincidences is a necessary process of scientific discovery; and coincidences between astronomic and atmospheric phenomena should be observed and noted. We know nothing of physical causes except by observing instances of what appear to be invariable and necessary sequence. After a certain amount of experience we assume the invariability and the necessity, and we do so most readily when one set of experiences is backed up and supported by other sets of experiences. The observation of sufficient coincidences in number may justify the acceptance of an empirical law according to which we may, with approximate safety, predict that when one of the events happens, the other will accompany or follow. To get beyond a merely empirical law of this kind, we require the support of another series of inductions or of as many more as we can obtain."

9.03—SUNSPOT OBSERVATIONS INADEQUATE TO TRACE FUNDAMENTAL CAUSES:

Observations of sunspots alone will never lead to the discovery of the laws which regulate the weather. The atmosphere is often liable to unusual and long continuing impressions, and these are induced by planetary action on the earth as well as on the photosphere of the Sun. Researches covering many years have indicated that the maximum frequency of sunspots coincides with the perihelion stations of Jupiter midway in the zodiacal sign Aries at cycles of 11.9 years, when excessive drought and atmospheric static are observed, temperatures are above the normal average and the rate of mortality is high. Great frost precede these droughts. The last perihelion of Jupiter occurred on March 15, 1928. The minimum frequency of sunspots appears to coincide with the aphelion station of Jupiter and last occurred in 1934. At such periods negative electricity reaches a maximum in the atmosphere, temperatures are below the normal average; an abnormally high average of precipitation with corresponding decrease in the rate of mortality have both been noted. The effects in either case may be somewhat modified or accentuated by the magnetic action of other planets which may be in configuration (negative aspects especially) either with Jupiter. The perigee, and perihelion passages of Uranus, Neptune, Saturn and Mars are specially important in this respect.

9.04—ABNORMALITIES OF WEATHER ACCOMPANIES OUTBREAKS OF DISEASE:

In order to discover the true cause of influenza we must look beyond the changes of weather which have so frequently preceded or accompanied the outbreak.   4-23-'38

Sudden variations of temperature and unusual weather for the season, in the opinion of astro-meteorologists, is due to the rare conjunctions, oppositions or quadratures of the superior planets as of chief importance among other planetary phenomena, as noted during the serious epidemics of 1917-18 and during 1926 when the superior planets Neptune, Saturn and Jupiter formed such angles to each other. During February, 1930 the square between Saturn and Uranus from Capricorn to Aries, was accompanied by abnormal atmospheric conditions that coincided with reports of pandemic disease. Occurring from cardinal signs, this configuration indicated periodical sharp outbreaks rather than a steady development of unusual weather or health conditions induced by the Saturn and

Uranus combination. Again, during July of that year, the opposition between Jupiter and Saturn was again accompanied by unhealthy atmospheric conditions. Regarding planetary action on weather the modus operandi is presumed to be electrical.

9.05—ELECTRICAL STATE OF THE ATMOSPHERE:

The prevalence of epidemic or pestilential disease has been associated with the absence or deficiency of positive electricity in the atmosphere; and mortality has been found to be in the inverse ratio of the amount of positive electricity with which the air is charged. In the non-electric states of the air, or when the electricity is below par normal, diseases of a low type prevail and the mortality increases. On the contrary, when the electricity is positive, strongly positive and active throughout the day, as is usual under the solar-Jupiter configurations which are conducive to increased ozone and descending air currents, the number of deaths decreases. Every planet has its individual signature. Mars, which inclines to evaporation and energizing the red ray in the solar spectrum, may induce extremes in this direction, resulting in excessive heat waves as are anticipated by its North Tropic position during the summer of 1938. Under such impulses eruptive diseases accompany the abnormal heat and dryness. Neptune effects are difficult to diagnose. Glandular systems seemingly respond. Uranus reacts on motor nerves. Saturn depresses through cold and excessive moisture as during the winter of 1934 when in February record low temperatures were reported. Jupiter appears to be associated with the respiratory system and reactions on the blood stream.

9.06—VOLCANIC ERUPTIONS AND EARTHQUAKES ACCOMPANIED BY OUTBREAKS OF DISEASE:

The frequency of the coincidence of volcanic eruptions and earthquakes with the outbreaks of epidemics, tends to support the hypothesis of planetary action being the exciting cause of all these phenomena, and electricity may be the agent. Among our astro-meteorological forecasts for 1926 as published exclusively in the Brooklyn (N.Y.) Citizen, November 15, 1925, we pointed out that the year following would be notable for seismic and volcanic disturbances, which in turn would affect conditions of health in various parts of the world. During the year 1926 Vesuvius became unusually active. Volcanic eruptions in the Far East and in the Pacific were recorded. Epidemic diseases broke out over restricted areas during the summer of 1926 when the planet Mars, attaining its perihelion station, was a contributory exciting factor. During the latter part of July, record heat waves covered the Eastern States and temperatures rose to 102 degrees similarly as on August 6, 1918. Typhus in pandemic form was reported from China and Italy on August 20, 1926. Jupiter was then applying to a square aspect of Saturn after separating from an opposition to Neptune, which was retrograde in motion. Usually, the effects of such slow moving planets endure for months after the culmination of the negative configurations. The aspects between Saturn and Uranus during February, 1930, between Jupiter and Saturn (opposition) during the summer following, and again when Saturn squared Uranus on December 12, 1930, were also productive of peculiar weather and health conditions that gave weather scientists and health authorities something to ponder over. At cycles of fifteen years, when Mars in perigee attains its closest proximity to the earth, outbreaks of smallpox and eruptive diseases appear to reach peaks of activity.

4-30-'38

9.07—STATISTICAL DATA:

Pythagoras gave the number of death as 17. Records show that Asiatic Cholera has been most generally prevalent at 17 year periods approximately. Pearce's Text-book of Astrology mentions that, according to Ling, during 173 years, from 287 to 460, nineteen distinct plagues occurred at intervals of 17 years, some continuing two or three years together. Coming down to modern times we might cite 1832-1849-1866-1883-1900 and 1917. Investigation discloses that the adverse configurations of the more ponderous planets appear to converge at or near these cyclic periods. For instance, during August, 1917, Saturn and Neptune formed a conjunction in the sign Leo. Saturn in Leo symbolizes the bones of the spine. This planet's conjunction with Neptune suggested devitalization of spinal fluids. There followed epidemics of spinal meningitis, also infantile paralysis (Saturn-Neptune), Leo being the sign having dominion over the heart and also exerting an influence over children (5th principle). These combined influences coincided with an unusually high death rate from heart troubles. Jupiter had previously squared Uranus during the preceding May from Taurus 23.00 to Aquarius 23.00, thus signaling through abnormal atmospheric conditions a prior effect on the respiratory systems and blood streams of those in whose natal charts these configurations affected sensitive points. Weather conditions affect respiration appreciably and investigation will show that people breathe deeper during the development of high pressure areas when descending air currents carry a larger proportion of ozone downward from higher air stratas to the surface, than when low pressure areas and excessive humid weather when ascending air currents are deficient of oxygen. The lack of oxygen, if continued over a long period eventually affects the blood stream and lowers the resistance of the body to resist spreading disease. Easterly winds, which by the way, are under the dominion of Saturn, have been observed to prevail coincidental with outbreaks of grippe and influenza. The wind then moves in a direction contrary to the rotary motion of the earth, which is from west to east. These easterly winds are unwholesome in every part of the world.

9.09—EPIDEMICS APPEAR TO MOVE FROM EAST TO WEST:

On October 1, 1918, Saturn, in Leo 24.14 formed an opposition to Uranus. As this configuration is very slow in forming the affects would begin to operate some time before the actual culmination of the aspect. On August 11 preceding, the Sun formed a conjunction with Saturn and on August 19 opposed Uranus. This period very likely brought to focus the most potent influences of the major opposition. And so, according to statistical records, the great influenza epidemic during the World War had its American start in Boston the first week of September, 1918 and by the end of the month virtually the entire nation was affected. Viewing this matter from another astrological angle it is noteworthy to mention that the radical Moon in the radical horoscope of the United States is situated in Aquarius 24.17. Uranus was transiting this point, opposed by Saturn when the epidemic broke out in this country: Saturn and Uranus will be affecting the same point by square aspect from Taurus during 1941-42—Uranus from Taurus 24.17 on April 13, 1941 and Saturn from the same degree on March 19, 1942. Moreover, a conjunction of Jupiter and Uranus will fall in Taurus 26.39 on May 8, 1941. A preceding conjunction of Jupiter and Saturn will fall in Taurus 9.06 on February 15, 1941. These configurations in and from the fixed and earthy sign Taurus will be emblematic not only of enduring abnormal weather conditions but also indicate a period of unusual seismic activity, and spectacular magnetic displays in May, 1941 under the Jupiter-Uranus conjunction. Effects should be most potent in those parts of the world where the conjunction falls in the upper or lower meridian or in 90 degree angles thereto, as indicated in the Aries Solar ingress for March, 1941. However, in view of the important transits to the radical Moon of the U.S. Horoscope, effects in this country should be duly considered.

Discussion of affects of these phenomena on economic conditions does not come under the subject of our present inquiry, but such consideration deserve equally serious study for mundane prognoses.

5-21-'38

10

THE SUN AND SOLAR ECLIPSES CONSIDERED

"Let there be lights in the firmament of heaven to divide the day from the night, and let them be for Signs and Seasons, and for Days".
—(Gen. 1:14)

10.01—GENERAL:

The Sun, which represents the dynamic heart principle in all signatures, imparts vital heat to creation. It is not necessary to explain in detail how solar heat directs the machinery of the atmosphere as the Sun traces its course along the ecliptic from extreme south declination to extreme north declination and vice versa, and regulates the normal variations of seasons and temperatures every year. "Old Sol" operates not only as the administrator of seasons but also as the day hand of the celestial timepiece as conjunctions and various aspects are formed with other heavenly arbiters. We might term the Sun the celestial generator, for when the Sun comes to the conjunction of any planet, the influence of such body is generated very generally in the atmosphere and the effects may be expected to manifest at any place of observation within three days after the exact conjunction. The parallel of declination is equally effective but also consider the angle of aspect coinciding with the parallel. The time of year when influences of the major planets will be most potent may be determined by the Sun's conjunction with each one.

10.02—Conjunctions of the Sun with Neptune fall about two to three days later each year; with Uranus, approximately five days later; with Saturn about eleven days later, and with Jupiter about a month later annually. As the orbital revolution of Mars is 687 days, conjunctions of the Sun with this red planet take place on an average of twenty-two months. Effects of these conjunctions on weather will therefore culminate at a different time each year and maximum influences will manifest over entirely different geographical areas each time, and principally where the planets are on the geographical

96

meridian. Observations indicate that, for the same season each year, there is an annual westward drift of between 75 and 87 degrees where extremes of weather characterized by the slowest moving planets are manifested.

Atmospheric disturbances are intensified when the Sun forms aspects with two or more planets of opposite natures or while mutual aspects accompany its configurations.

10.03—ERECTING INGRESS CHARTS:
Before venturing interpretations of weather, charts of the heavens should be erected for the beginning of the respective seasons, at the place of observation. These charts represent the primary keys to weather prognoses, since the 4th house represents the Earth's attractive virtue at any point for which the chart is transposed. Planets in the 4th or 10th are of chief importance. Those in the 3rd or 9th houses indicate general weather conditions immediately westward of the observer. The Sun's ingress into Aries rules the Spring quarter; in Cancer, the Summer quarter; into Libra, the Autumnal season; and into Capricorn, affords index of the general character of the Winter season. In order to trace causes of earthquakes, droughts, and other major causes which are known to follow eclipses when eclipse degrees are excited by transits in conjunction, opposition or square by major planets, it is advisable to carefully calculate and study charts of eclipses, or keep a file of degrees in which eclipses have occurred three years past or a few years ahead. (Refer to Moon's North Node). Note also when major planets are in the celestial equator of tropics, as periods when unusual weather conditions may be expected.

10.04—EQUINOCTIAL STORMS:
The popular idea that equinoctial storms coincide with the Sun's passage over the celestial equator at the equinoxes is not supported by practical observations. Our own experiences indicate that the relative positions of the planets at or near the time of the Sun's equinoxes are largely the causes of such atmospheric phenomena, particularly if any celestial bodies then occupy the early degrees of cardinal signs. The equinox of Uranus in 1927, of Saturn in 1938 and Neptune in 1943-44 were primarily related to anomalies of weather during those periods. And so likewise with Uranus in the North Tropic during the fall of 1948 and the summer of 1949. It has also been observed that when the North Node occupies the sign Aries, the effects of hurricanes in the northern hemisphere are more potent.

The elementary student of astro-meteorology should begin by studying the Sun's conjunctions, oppositions, squares and parallels for negative influences weatherwise. The sextiles and trines should be noted for positive influences. Three to four days should be allowed after the culmination of a solar aspect for indicated character of weather to manifest. Also by noting when major planets are stationary or in the north tropic, the student becomes familiar with the general character of planets as related to atmospheric changes.

10.05—ECLIPSES:

Eclipses of the Sun may be total, annular or partial. Effects vary according to whether they fall in fire, earth, air, water, human or bestial signs. Interpretations are derived from positions of eclipses falling in any of the 36 decans of 10 degrees. A Chaldean cycle is the period between any given eclipse and its return, and consists of 18 years, 10 days, 7 hours and 42 minutes. The eclipses are visible in the same place after 54 years 1 month. The eclipse of the Sun on January 24, 1925 at 9:45 A.M., E.S.T., in Aquarius 4° 08' was visible in the United States. Add 18 years and 11 days and we reach February 4, 1943, 6:30 p.m. E.S.T. when an eclipse in Aquarius 15°16' was visible eight hours or 120 degrees westward.*

Voluminous statistics compiled by A.J. Pearce, Sepharial, John Hazelrigg and other learned investigators confirm Ptolemy's admonitions that eclipses are the forerunners of earthquakes, droughts, famines, inundations, epidemics and other major causes, including political mutations or wars. It is due in large measure to neglecting eclipse charts that many astrologers have injected hypothetical points and unscientific theories to account for disasters of great magnitude.

10.06—METONIC CYCLE:

The Metonic cycle dates back to Meton, a Greek astronomer, born about 460 B.C., who made the discovery that nineteen solar years are equal in length to 235 lunar months, so that at the end of the cycle the phases of the moon recur on the same day of the month. It will be noted therefore that eclipses of the Sun are sometimes repeated in the same degree of the same zodiacal sign and on the same date exactly nineteen years later.

Referring to eclipses of the Sun in the first decan of Taurus

---

*We commend to the reader for serious study and reference, Sepharial's book <u>Eclipses in Theory and Practice</u>, Chapters VIII, IX and X for interpretations of both solar and lunar eclipses.

being related to droughts and injury to crops, A.J. Pearce, in his Textbook of Astrology, Vol. II, p. 61, writes: "It cannot be 'mere coincidence' that Zadkiel I. foretold, from the planetary positions at the annular eclipse of the Sun in Taurus 5⁰ 04', of April 25, 1846, 'drought, failure of the fruits of the earth, and some peculiar disease in potatoes,' and that Ireland and Scotland then suffered from these evils to such an extent that thousands were starved..." (Vide Zadkiel's Almanac, 1846, pp. 15,34, published a year before the event).

It may be noteworthy to mention here that the first decan of the earthy sign Taurus relates to starchy products such as potatoes, corn, etc.

On April 28, 1930, at 2:07 p.m., E.S.T., an eclipse of the Sun took place in Taurus 7 45'. The Moon's North Node was then in Taurus 2° 43'. The drought and resulting dust storms in our Western States following this eclipse and the consequent crop failures are a matter of historical record. An Associated Press dispatch from Montgomery, Ala., that was published in the New York World, Sept. 27, 1930, reported that 130,000 Alabama farm tenants and their families faced destitution because of the summer drought and the prevailing low prices of farm products. Mars was in transit over the degree of the eclipse on June 13. Jupiter, at maximum north declination 23° 15' from June 25 to July 7, was opposing Saturn. In addition to these eclipses in Taurus being precursors of certain unusual weather conditions they—not the North Node as some of the cycle experts deduce—are important time factors in relation to changing economic trends.

Exactly nineteen years later, on April 28, 1949, 3:03 A.M., E.S.T. another eclipse of the Sun falls in Taurus 7° 43'. The North Node will then occupy Aries 25° 15', with Mercury in 23° 36' and Mars in 28° 40' of the same sign. Twelve days after the eclipse, Mars will transit the eclipse degree. With Uranus in the 4th house in Gemini 27° 44' and close to the North Tropic, the deduction is obvious. The Sun arrives at the place of Uranus in this chart on Jure 19, 1949.

11

THE MOON AND THE LUNAR QUARTERS

11.01—<u>GENERAL</u>:

The Moon, besides ruling the tides by its risings, settings and transits over the meridian, is a most important timing element in governing the <u>distribution</u> of moisture in Nature. This lesser light indicates variations of humidity and barometric pressure as, in passing the key chart meridian of any geographical area or magnetic angles thereto, it reflects the qualities of planets with which it has formed a conjunction or other aspect. It moves round the Earth in 27½ days, causing weather conditions to move from west to east (anti-clockwise in the chart) at an average rate of 13 degrees of terrestrial longitude per day. Sometimes the movement is retarded and at other times atmospheric phenomena may seemingly remain stationary for a few days when high and low pressure areas converge.

Note carefully those days when the Moon transits the lower meridian (north) or upper meridian (south) and observe in the <u>ingress</u> chart the combinations of qualities it has accumulated from planets over points west of your place of observation. Thus may be understood why weather conditions in any locality are dependent upon existing atmospheric phenomena and prevailing winds in adjacent areas. If the Moon transits the Midheaven, the prevailing weather condition is centralized over southern parts; if through the 4th, the high or low pressure movement is tracing a path in northern parts. Similarly, make note of the Moon's transits over the ascendant or descendant, or midway between any of these four points. These aspects bring to manifestation the seven and three-and-a-half day cycles of changes during periods of freak weather, i.e., when major planets hold important positions. Note further those days when the Moon is in perigee, in the celestial equator, or in maximum north declination as periods of excessive humidity and barometric pressure, hence tending to intensify existing atmospheric disturbances.

11.02—<u>LUNAR QUARTERS</u>:

Even as the four ingresses of the Sun into cardinal signs during the year divide the seasons and afford interpretations of the general character of the atmosphere for season, so likewise do charts for the lunar phases with their attendant phenomena provide <u>particulars</u> concerning modifying weather indications for each week. These charts, with respect to the relative positions of planets, should be judged similarly as ingress charts. Effects of a planet near the meridian in an ingress chart are intensified when it holds the same position in a lunar quarter map.

The principle is as consistent and practical in the lunar charts as in the solar quarters, though apparently overlooked by many observers. The changing phases of the Moon do not, as commonly supposed, change the character of the weather. It is rather the relative positions of planets to the geographical meridian that indicate such changes. For example, Uranus <u>in the zodiacal sign</u> occupying the meridian at a lunar quarter tends to higher barometric pressure and lower temperatures for the week; Saturn, on the other hand inclines to easterly winds, lower barometer and leaden skies. Mars indicates more evaporation than usual and rising temperatures; Venus conduces to mild, humid atmosphere, southerly winds and temperate showers. Jupiter, with north winds, fine growing weather. Mercury is indicative of breezy atmosphere and variable winds. Neptune imparts misty air, variable winds, sometimes static and causing smoke fogs. Changeable and squally. If Venus transits, there may be flash floods.

Observations indicate that the <u>Moon's declination</u> determines the changing paths of atmospheric conditions moving eastward. The declinations of the planets should also be duly considered. South declinations exert more potent influences in the southern hemisphere.

11.03—<u>PERIGEE</u>:

The Moon at perigee is 221,464 miles distant from the earth. At the apogee, its distance is 252,715 miles. According to Dr. George Howard Darwin, for over thirty years professor of astronomy at Cambridge University, "the Moon's perigee effect on tides is 30 per cent greater then the apogee effect." Correspondingly, therefore, the humidity should be approximately 30 per cent greater at perigee than at apogee.

When the Moon's position in the <u>equator</u> or extreme <u>north declination</u> occurs at the same time as the New Moon in <u>perigee</u>, the greatest disturbances to which our earth is liable may then be expected with certainty of fulfillment. Snowstorms at such periods are apt to be driven and drifted by high velocity winds.

During the year 1947 the Moon's perigee each month coincided very close to the maximum north declination, generating everything from freak snowstorms in the winter and spring, to tornadoes and flash floods in connection with which we have maintained a diary from which to compile future reference data. Most critical was the lunation on July 17 with the Moon in perigee end maximum north declination.

A methodical system of reference is to draw a graph of the Moon's daily declination, allowing for 28° 45' north and south of the center (equator) line. Then insert the perigee points under the proper dates, together with planetary phenomena.

11.04—MOON IN CELESTIAL EQUATOR:
The tides rise highest at the conjunction and opposition of the Moon when the Sun is near the equinoctial points (Aries and Libra). The barometer is more apt to be depressed. On October 2, 1929, in New York, when the conjoined luminaries opposed the planet Uranus in Aries 9° 25'R, the tides in the harbor rose so high that ferry services between New York and New Jersey were temporarily suspended.

A Full Moon or New Moon near the equinoxes greatly intensifies prevailing storms and invites seismic shocks, owing to the strong tidal pull exerted by both luminaries upon the earth.

11.05—MOON'S POSITION DURING EARTHQUAKES:
Dr. Harland T. Stetson, while engaged in cosmic terrestrial research at Massachusetts Institute of Technology, studied some two thousand major earthquakes in Japan and the Philippines and found that there is a connection between the time of earthquakes and the position of the Moon.

It appears that earthquakes take place most frequently when the Moon is exerting its pull in a <u>horizontal direction</u>. The connection between the two phenomena was particularly striking in the case of 150 deep focus earthquakes. This is interesting in view of our astrological theory that the horizontal line drawn from the ascendant to the descendant in a chart is emblematic of the equator and the vertical line of the meridian is symbolic of the tropics.

(Refer to 4.06 for chart of the Los Angeles earthquake, with comments on the moon's position. Also refer to 8.05.)

11.06—<u>NEOMENIA</u>:
Although Ptolemy, Hally and Pearce emphasize the need for referring to the new or full Moon nearest the Aries ingress for judgment of the weather, it appears that they ignored other seasons in this instruction. A lunation, except there be an eclipse, covers a period of only one month. A solar ingress, on the other hand, has dominion over a season. During many years of checking modern weather maps which show the prevailing weather conditions daily all over the United States, our experiences indicate that the Moon, as a time marker, operates more successfully when applied to ingress charts. Lunar quarter maps are then supplemented for weekly periods though invariably referred to the ingress map as the primary key to weather prognosis.

11.07—<u>THUNDERSTORMS</u>:
A.J. Pearce supports Dr. Goad's opinion that thunderstorms rarely <u>begin</u> when the Moon is above the horizon.

12

THE MOON'S NORTH NODE AS
AN IMPORTANT CYCLIC FACTOR

12.01—GENERAL:

The Moon's Nodes are the two points where the plane of the Sun's orbit and that of the Moon cross each other. The North or Ascending Node is the point at which the Moon crosses the Sun's path in its passage from south to north. The South or Descending Node is that at which the Moon passes from the north to the south of the Sun's orbital plane.

It is only when the Sun and Moon form a conjunction or opposition, that is, when there is either a new or full Moon at or close to the Node, that there can be an eclipse. There can be no eclipse of the Sun when that luminary is more than 18° 31' from the Node. Nor can there be an eclipse of the Moon when, at opposition to the Sun, it is more than 12°15' from the Node.

Some years ago Raphael contended that the nodes are "nothing" and that as "neither a planet nor the shadow of the planet exists where they are," they can produce no effect whatsoever. On the other hand Wynn, in August 1936, published an article on the subject of "Nodes and Real Estate Values." However, since the Nodes indicate the approximate positions on the ecliptic where eclipses take place, it is reasonable to believe that many of the influences attributed to the Nodes are in fact the effects of eclipses. Eclipses, not the nodal points, are recognized in the phenomena of major causes and it has been demonstrated by statistical data that transits of superior planets to the conjunction, opposition or square of the degrees of eclipses and not the Nodes are the true timing factors of effects from the eclipses, apart from attendant planetary phenomena. Some of the interpretations inferred from Nodes are based on conjectural opinions alone and only serve to mislead students. Indeed, in reading a recently published astrological article referring to a physiological subject, we were amused to note that the author had ascribed a certain physiological condition due to the eclipse of the Sun having taken place close to the Moon's Node!

The Nodes should be inserted in all astrotechnical charts to indicate the proximity of eclipses. Neglecting to duly consider and insert sensitive eclipse degrees in charts has resulted in the development of various and sundry hypothetical positions to account for effects. The Nodes are, nevertheless, vitally important as cyclic factors, especially in mundane or weather prognoses.

12.02—EFFECTS ON MOON'S DECLINATION:

We are presently concerned with the North or Ascending Node which, by its position, indicates the cyclic variation in the maximum declination of the Moon. The North Node, with an annual motion of 19° 20', retrograding through the signs, returns to the same zodiacal position after 18.6 years or approximately 18 years and 31 weeks. When the North Node reaches Aries 0° (as in 1932 and in 1950), and the Moon is 90 degrees in advance of the Node, the Moon's declination extends to the absolute maximum of 28° 45'. At or near this period, the Moon exerts its maximum influence on barometric pressure and on high average of precipitation, especially at times of the Moon in perigee. As the North Node retrogrades through Pisces and other signs the maximum declination decreases until the North Node reaches Libra 0° which corresponds to the period in which the Moon's maximum declination recedes to 18° 10', and the Moon exerts its minimum influence on barometric pressure and on rainfall in the northern hemisphere. The conditions are just the reverse in the southern hemisphere under each signature. Then, for a period of 9.3 years, as the North Node retrogrades from Libra to Aries, the Moon's maximum declination increases. These variations in maximum declination have been found, after many years of practical observations, to affect the movements of ocean surface tides all over the world and result in rhythmic climatic changes.

Our observations seem to indicate that when maximum declinations extend above the Tropic of 23° 27', storm centers correspondingly follow more northern paths and that when they recede toward the maximum of 18° 10' storm tracks following more southerly courses.

12.03—BIBLIOGRAPHY:

Investigations of this subject by Abbe Gabriel, Prof. of Mathematics, of the University of Caen, France; Father Ricard, astronomer of Santa Clara University, Calif; Herbert Janvrin Browne, climatologist, late of Washington, D.C., and other scientific noteworthies have yielded instructive knowledge of astro-meteorological interest regarding the cyclic value of the North Node as amply supported by voluminous graphs and statistical data. Their findings indicate the vital importance of the North Node in relation to fluctuating tidal movements in all oceans, with resulting effects not only on average temperatures, distribution of moisture, varying intensity of hurricane phenomena and seismic activity, but also reflecting through political and economic trends.

During the last several years, several books and pamphlets on cyclic trends stressed this 18.6 year cycle as seemingly newly discovered to indicate both cyclic weather and economic trends, but which fail to consider either eclipses or important planetary phenomena. It may be noteworthy to mention here that, with due respect to any cycles whatsoever, positions of superior planets in certain signs, in the celestial equator of tropics, or when on the meridian in any ingress chart, are likewise related to unusual conditions of weather. Furthermore, when nearly all the major planets are in north declination they exert greater effects on the northern hemisphere, and vice versa when the majority are in south declination. Thus declination affords one of the primary keys to the geographical latitude wherein effects may be expected.

Sir John Hershel, in his remarks on "The Weather" in Good Words, January, 1864, commented that an eminent meteorologist, Luke Howard, employed a weather cycle of nineteen years, based on the circulation of the Moon's Node and also took into account the Moon's varying maximum declination as influencing the averages of rainfall, and the height of the barometer. During the World War II some of the cycle experts apparently made interesting discoveries of theories that have been waiting nearly a century to be exploited in book form, without giving credit to the source or origin. A.J. Pearce directed attention to the subject in 1885. It is amusing how science is gradually applying long recognized astrological rules under other nomenclatures.

12.04—STATISTICAL DATA:
Among some theories advanced after statistical studies of the Nodes were the following.

(a) At Fort Hamilton, N.Y. covering a period of 29 years from 1893 to 1922, variations of mean high water to mean sea level indicated by a reversible graph that high water levels increase from the North node's position in Libra 0^0 until it reaches Aries 0^0. They then recede until the node reaches Libra 0°. With the Node in Libra the tides are depressed 2.39 feet <u>below</u> mean sea level. When the Node is in Aries, the elevation of mean high water is 2.30 feet <u>above</u> mean sea level. As the North Node passes through the north tropic the elevation of the tides is approximately normal. When the full Moon occurs at or close to its perigee, the tides are unusually high.

(b) Indian famines are greatest when the node is near Aries 0°.

(c) Cold winters in the United States (tabulating 63 cold winters) indicate highest average when the <u>North Node</u> was in the quadrants from Libra to Cancer and from Capricorn to Libra, with highest frequency when approximate to Libra.

(d) Inundations were 67.5 greater when the North Node occupied the quadrants from Cancer to Aries and more intense with great storms coincident with full Moons of September, October, November and December when the full Moon was near its perigee or the Earth was near perihelion. These have been periods of extremely high tides with corresponding low barometric pressure.

(e) Abbe Gabriel has pointed out that "the principal idea that dominates all meteorological research is the common ground between astronomical and atmospheric phenomena. This idea is as old as humanity.... Seashore dwellers had rightly attributed the phenomena of the tides to the Moon many centuries before astronomers were able to give it scientific explanation.... The influence of the Moon on the weather, so much discussed in history by learned men, cannot be denied without temerity.... When one studies this question open mindedly, the student should discover that nearly all the lunar phases, counting from the beginning of new Moon, correspond to a particular type of weather, marked by the respective locations of atmospheric highs and lows."

(Modern science is gradually recognizing fragments of the rules set forth by the renowned Ptolemy in his <u>Tetrabiblos</u> nearly eighteen centuries ago)—G.J.McC.

(f) During the Spring of 1947, Uranus was on the lower meridian at Long. 90° West, thus indicating an abnormally cool and stormy Spring season in the Midwest and Central United States, with some effects in the Eastern States. The Moon in perigee on March 29, April 24, May 22 and June 19, in each instance coincided closely with the Moon in maximum north declination. Devastating hurricanes in the Texas-Oklahoma Panhandle, in Kansas and Missouri as well as record low readings in the barometer in Cleveland, OH and at Buffalo, New York were ample verification of these signatures in that geographical zone where Uranus induced anomalous weather.

APPENDIX

DROUGHTS:

Severe droughts through the strategic Greet Plains region occurred in 1889, in 1890, in 1894, in 1901, in 1910, in 1917, in 1930, 1931, 1934 (dust storms) and in 1936.

Drought periods often turn the fertile Central Plains into a huge dust bowl, burning up crops. Experience shows these prolonged periods of drought most likely to occur in the winter or autumn, least likely in summer. In 1910 a desert climate existed in most of the Southern Plains and much of the Northern Plains, extending eastward as far as Wisconsin.

As a clue to the 1934 drought, the Moon's perigee was then falling each month in Capricorn, close to the Moon's maximum south declination and the southern hemisphere was getting most of the precipitation. In July, 1934, Mars was in the north tropic, attaining maximum north declination July 18-19.

For further index we should revert to the solar ingresses of March 21 and June 21, checking positions of planets near the meridian at Long 90° West.

Found with the copy of the book from which this edition was taken.

July 7, 1947

Memo to Andrew L_____:

There have been numerous opinions expressed regarding various aspects to use in astrology, but in weather, which we have been able to observe daily, it is found that all operative aspects are based on multiples of 15 degrees. For example the conjunction and opposition (180⁰) are strongest of the aspects, but the Parallel of declination is stronger than either for positive effects. Next in strength are the square, sextile, trine, semi-sextile, 150 degrees, 45° and 135 degrees. I discount all other aspects. Orbs do not mean anything in weather. The aspect indicates the origin of weather. The positions in the charts on the meridian or in aspect thereto at any geographical meridian indicate the time.

The Moon principally affects the barometer and it's transit over the meridian at the place of observation or to the square or semi-square, are definite time factors. The Moon on the meridian usually carries weather to your place of observation in the ingress charts. Your ingress charts should be transposed for the longitude and latitude of Kingston, Pa., which is earlier than New York hence receives weather earlier, since weather moves from west to east.

I would suggest that you contact your nearest local weather bureau and ask if they will put you on their list for daily weather maps and for the monthly weather summary. By watching the Federal Weather maps you can check daily weather movements against your calculations. It might be a good plan to keep a daily diary of temperatures and weather locally, noting whether storms (lows) or cold clear weather (highs) move north or south of your place of observation, since these phenomena control wind directions and are instructive in relating wind direction to weather indications. Winds usually blow toward the center of storms. With respect to high pressure areas (or cool clear fronts) winds blow from their center.

It is well to study direction of winds as a key to approaching weather because when the wind sets in from the east with increasing cloudiness and lowering barometer, you may anticipate ten to twelve hours of this wind direction followed by a prolonged atmospheric disturbance lasting twelve to eighteen hours. Weather today at Chicago, usually affects Kingston the following day.

When storms are north of you the wind is blowing from the southeast before the storm, then from the south and after the storm passes east of you the wind veers to the southwest then west and northwest, followed by cooler weather. This is the usual pattern. But if storms pass south of you the wind is from the north and an appreciable fall in temperature may be anticipated.

It will be of interest to the coal operators to accumulate considerable stock piles of coal for next winter because the demand for fuel will be great throughout the eastern States. I anticipate the coldest winter in thirty years. You can pass this on to your local paper and may quote me if you like.

Gee Jay

P.S. Watch for the intensity of storms over July 17-18 when the New Moon falls in the 4th house of the Summer Solstice, with Moon in maximum north declination and IN PERIGEE. The Moon's effect is 30 per cent more potent when in perigee than in apogee. Storms range farther north than usual and tornadoes are more intense at these times. This combination over July 17-18 is a most unusual phenomenon.

Found with the copy of the book from which this edition was taken.

This is the draft of a page in the forthcoming Year Book and explains in detail what you may expect next winter.   G.J.McC   7-7-47

The Moon's Nodes
[*see pg. 99—Editor*] his <u>Textbook</u>, Vol.II, p. 61, writes: "it cannot be 'mere coincidence' that Zadkiel (Comdr. Morrison, R.N.) foretold, from the planetary positions at the annular eclipse of the Sun in Taurus 5^0 04', of April 25, 1846, 'drought, failure of the fruits of the earth, and some peculiar disease in potatoes', and that Ireland and Scotland then suffered from these evils to such an extent that thousands were starved..." (Vide <u>Zadkiel's Almanac</u>, 1846, pp. 15, 34, published nearly a year before the event).

It should be borne in mind that eclipses are not always pernicious. When falling on degrees in favorable aspect to benefics, they can indicate opportunities and benefits through others.

For purposes of astrological precision, account should be taken not only of eclipses, but also of solar ingresses, cardinal positions of superior planets and important configurations between those celestial bodies. From such phenomena may be sought major causes. For example, Uranus approaching the north tropic or maximum north declination during the next few years will contribute in no small measure to extremes of weather in the northern hemisphere. This indication will become more manifest over the eastern half of the United States during the severe winter of 1947-48, which may set new records for the past thirty years for low temperatures and snow depths. Mercury, at the Winter Solstice, will oppose Uranus on the lower meridian at Long. 78^0 West. The central line of the emergency zone passes northward approximately 30 miles west of Richmond, Va., across the Blue Ridge Mountains into Pennsylvania, through Central Pennsylvania, just east of Altoona, and just east of Batavia, N. Y. but including all Western New York in the zone of greatest intensity. Saturn in sextile to Uranus intensifies the cold and Mercury's aspect inclines to high velocity winds, driving snow in high drifts. Intense cold waves culminating in the interior from Cleveland and Columbus, Ohio and ranging eastward should follow snowstorms.

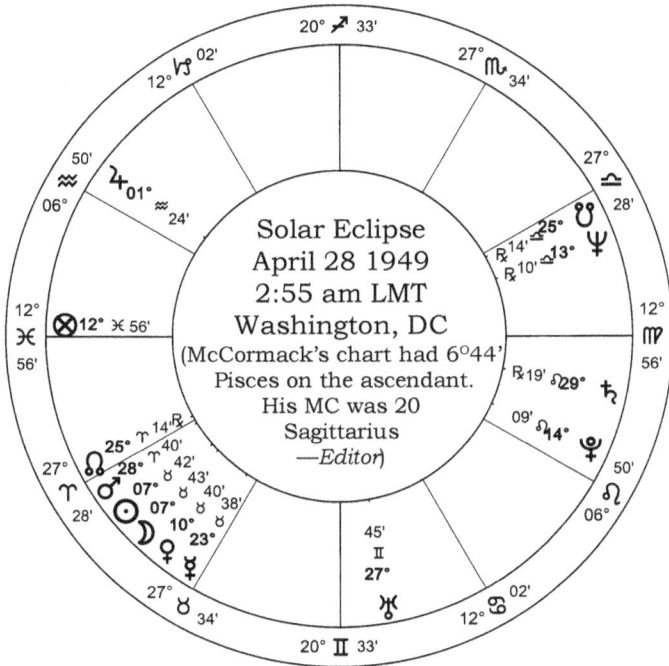

Solar Eclipse
April 28 1949
2:55 am LMT
Washington, DC
(McCormack's chart had 6°44'
Pisces on the ascendant.
His MC was 20
Sagittarius
—Editor)

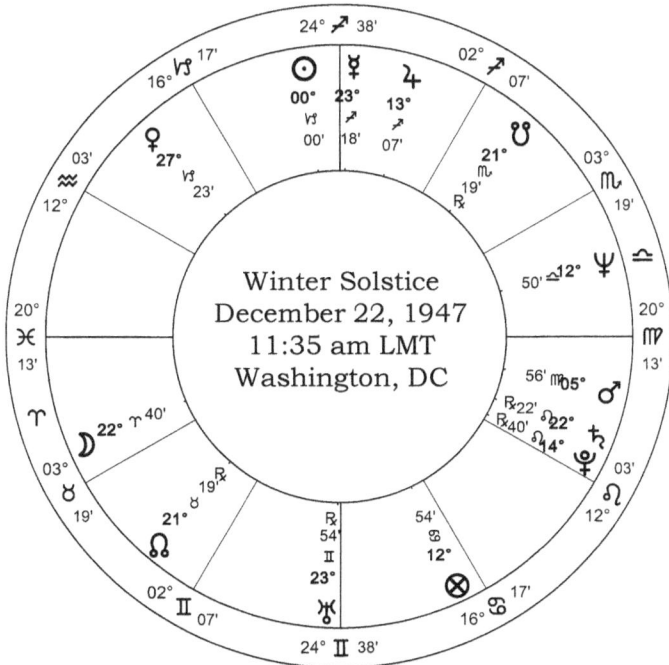

Winter Solstice
December 22, 1947
11:35 am LMT
Washington, DC

The 78th meridian indicated the zone of greatest property damage by storm and other emergencies, Uranus is the primary indicator of locality and time. Observe those dates when any planets oppose, square or conjoin this position of Uranus. Note also those dates when the Moon conjoins, squares, or opposes Uranus as timing these phenomena to the 78th meridian, thence eastward. Note periods of greatest intensity and barometric pressure when the Moon is in <u>perigee</u> and near maximum north declination. A "white" Christmas in 1947 is indicated for the Mid-Atlantic and Eastern States. Magnetic storms may be anticipated on or about February 6, 1948 and again during mid-November, 1948. The Mercury-Uranus configuration is a potential blizzard breeder, though extremes may not be expected until northwest gales originate from the vicinity of Toronto, Canada on December 23. Maximum intensity of the high barometric pressure conducing to extremes of low temperatures may be expected during the first week of March when both Uranus and Mercury attain apparent stationary positions.

Found with the copy of the book from which this edition was taken.

George J. McCormack
Fair Lawn, New Jersey

July 7, 1947

Mr. A. L....
Kingston, Pa

Dear Mr. L____,
This will acknowledge receipt of your letter dated July 3, with enclosure of U.S. postal Note for $5.00 in prepayment for a copy of Astrotech Weather Guide.

The Weather Guide is not just another book. It eliminates all hitherto conjectural theories and the principles expounded are based on more than thirty-three years of personal observations and profound studies of this subject in which I have majored. I feel confident that this is the most complete brochure on the subject yet published. Everything is boiled down to essentials, suitably indexed for ready reference.

It is contained in a three ring loose leaf binder, 8½ X 11 so that additional pages may be later inserted in their appropriate places in each lesson. My interest in subscribers does not end with their subscription to the book. From time to time I will endeavor to collaborate with them in connection with weather observations and thus encourage a keener interest in this branch of astrology.

Since I have made recent additions to the book but have not mimeographed the additional pages to date, it has been necessary for me to type them. I did not expect orders to be coming in so soon but will have your book in the mail before the end of this week.

For your information, the Winter Solstice of next December, which I have referred to in the forthcoming Year Book, will be of special interest to your locality, since you may expect one of the severest and snowiest winters in years throughout northern Pennsylvania. The season should set some long standing records for low temperatures, while the following Spring should be characterized by serious floods in the Susquehanna, Potomac, Ohio, Allegheny and other Eastern Rivers. Would advise people to stock up early and plentifully with fuel for next winter. Uranus will be on the lower meridian at Long 87 west, which crosses northward through Altoona, affecting Pittsburgh but moreso northern Pennsylvania and Western New York. Snowfall should be heavy. I will write more about this later.

Thanking you again for your order and hoping that you will find the Weather Guide an inspiration to serious study, I am,

Faithfully,

"Gee Jay"

115

Found with the copy of the book from which this edition was taken. The clipping was not dated, nor is the name of the paper known.

HOT SUMMER IS FORECAST

Sultry, Humid Weather Ahead, McCormack Says

Fair Lawn, N. J., June 25—(AP)—Long range weather forecaster George J. McCormack, who predicted last winter's big snow months before it came, says this summer's weather will be awful,

"The weather will vary from hot and dry with excessive humidity preceding local squalls, even to cloudbursts, and subsequent sharp declines in temperatures from Aug. 19 to Aug. 22," he calmly announced yesterday.

"One of the principal features of the summer season," he continued fearlessly, "will be sultry, humid weather, prevalent haze or low cloudiness over the eastern third of the country."

McCormack, who does it all by astro-meteorology, said the season's best vacation weather would be during the third week of July, the first two weeks of August up to Aug. 18 and the second week in September.

The next few days, McCormack said, will be difficult. His charts show the current heat wave is here to stay a while.

"Some of the hottest weather is scheduled for the end of June into the opening days of July from Mississippi Valley westward to the Continental Divide and in the Southwest. But the heat wave will be broken during the second week of July, about July 11-12."

"On July 4 holiday weekend," McCormack concluded, "thunderstorms and local squalls originating in the Mississippi Valley on the 2nd will move Eastward toward the Atlantic from July 3 to July 5. These storms will be followed by clearing and cooler weather of a type better suited to indoor activities."

RELEASE: September 28, 1947
George J. McCormack
Fair Lawn, New Jersey
September 22, 1947

SEVERE WINTER INDICATED FOR MID-ATLANTIC AND EASTERN STATES

The winter of 1947-48 over Mid-Atlantic and Eastern States, beginning on December 22, 1947, is indicated as being the most severe in thirty years, with regard to low ranges of temperatures, high wind velocities and accumulative snowfall. These unusual atmospheric conditions should manifest from Minnesota, Iowa and Mississippi eastward, with the line of maximum intensity and "emergencies" ranging along the 78th meridian of west longitude, this is from Toronto, Canada; through Buffalo, N.Y, and vicinity, thence south through mid-Pennsylvania to include Pittsburgh on the western tangent of the zone. Along this zone the high pressure or cold front barometric areas from Canada should sweep arctic temperatures southward and then curve eastward with maximum effects in the highlands of the interior and along the Great Lakes through Western New York and northern New England. The 78th meridian indicates the central line of the zone where maximum property damage may be anticipated from the elements or other causes.

Buffalo, Rochester, Syracuse, Batavia and adjacent communities in Western New York, together with northern Pennsylvania, may expect to receive the maximum intensity of snowstorms progressing eastward. Intense cold waves, accompanied by high velocity winds from the northwest should range eastward from the Ohio Valley on the western tangent of snowstorms, with a "white Christmas" to usher in the official winter season. This may not be very comforting news for motorists or transportation companies that expect to use the northern highways during the holiday season. Nevertheless, the information affords making arrangements to avoid northern highway hazards. For long haul highway transportation, southern highways are recommended during this coming winter. State and municipal snow removal equipment should be in readiness for record

117

snowfalls with only a minimum of thaws. This implies wind drifted snow and hard packed surface accumulation along northern highways throughout the winter. The evening of December 26 should bring reports of the advancing cold blasts from the higher altitudes of the interior.

Movements of fuel oil and coal should be planned so that excess supplies may be stored in Eastern stock piles before December 22, as safeguards against delays in transit after that date. One of the most intense cold waves of the winter may be expected to originate on February 29 north of Toronto, Canada and sweep south and eastward through the first four days of March. A busy season for plumbers, fur goods, heavy winter clothing, automobile repairs, rubber goods, outdoor winter sports equipment and for heating equipment.

Magnetic storms, on or about February 6, may be ascribed to the combined actions of the planets Jupiter and Uranus in magnetic angles to this part of the globe.

The only comparison to our Winter in the eastern half of the United States may be reports of a cold and blustery winter from the southern areas of China, at approximately 103 degrees east longitude. Meanwhile, over the British Isles and Western Europe, opposite extremes of weather should be reported in abnormally high temperatures for the season and with accompanying minimum precipitation. With Mars in magnetic angle to those geographical areas and in closest approach to the earth in February, Western Europe may be boasting of "heat waves" during the second week of January. Maritime shipping in the eastern portion of the North Atlantic may experience rough weather, particularly during the second and last weeks of January.

During the next few years, until 1950, we pass through a quadrant in the 18.6 year weather cycle in which anomalies of atmospheric phenomena will be characterized by extremes of cold and heat throughout certain seasons. These conditions may be accounted for largely by movements of ocean surface currents as the absolute maximum declination of the Moon (28^0 45') is gradually approached, with accompanying maximum mean average of precipitation and maximum height of the barometric pressure.

Based on our thirty-three years of investigations of major and minor weather cycles, we have evolved a theory, confirmed by critical experimental forecasts for various parts of the world, indicating that certain extremes of weather for a season are manifested approximately 80 to 87 degrees westward in terrestrial longitude the following year. Furthermore, this theory appears to account for the wide differentials of temperatures or downfall existing in various geographical areas at one time. For example during the winter of 1946-47 subnormal temperatures and heavy snowfall affected the British Isles and western Europe, including Berlin, Germany. This coming winter, the "emergency" line falls on the meridian at Longitude 73 degrees West. During the winter of 1948-49 the same unusual weather should be indicated at Longitude 165 degrees West, or north of the Hawaiian Islands.

During the spring season of 1948, the Mid-Atlantic and Eastern States may experience an aftermath of accumulated snow and ice over northern areas after a severe winter. With a sudden thaw setting in suddenly under gentle southerly winds on and immediately following April 1, inundations of the Ohio, Monongahela, Allegheny, Susquehanna, Genesee, Connecticut and other eastern waterways may be anticipated.

A hot and dry summer season in 1948, with maximum intensity at the 83rd meridian of west longitude ranging from Columbus, north to Cleveland, OH, and progressing eastward, should compensate for the cold winter. Excessive temperatures during the first three weeks of July and the second week of September. Conserve water for the summer drought. On the West Coast downfall above the average and temperatures will range considerably lower, especially in the north.

At the Fall Equinox of 1948, beginning on September 22, the planet Uranus, in the north tropic for the first time in 84 years, predicates lower ranges of temperature than normal for the season throughout the northern hemisphere. The 80th meridian of west longitude indicates the central line of a storm area of maximum intensity. Cold in the interior and damp, cloudy weather in lowlands with preponderating easterlies.

It may be of interest to mention that, on February 22, 1947, as one of our experimental tests, at personal expense, we prepared and mailed forecasts to Bell Telephone Companies, to railroads, transportation companies and to a Midwest newspaper regarding the cold, wet and prolonged Spring of 1947. We definitely stated that the 90th meridian of west longitude would be the central line of an "emergency" zone and that late cold weather would require wearing of top coats as late as June 13-15. On June 12, at Sidney, Neb., six inches of snow was reported, with a minimum temperature of 32 degrees! At New York, meanwhile, a maximum temperature of 37.1 degrees was officially reported. Our forecast was published in a research bulletin and publicly distributed on February 22.

These astro-meteorological observations are derived solely from soli-lunar and planetary phenomena in connection with which astronomical charts, transposed for various terrestrial meridians afford the means of interpreting where planets in magnetic angles to the earth manifest maximum influences in affecting certain characters of atmospheric phenomena.

George J. McCormack, F.A.F.A,

The following was extracted from a longer article that was found with the copy of the book from which this edition was made. It was taken from Horoscope Magazine, *the year is 1963, the month unknown.* — *Editor.*

WEATHER ASTROLOGY YOU CAN USE

Influences of the Signs

ARIES. Temperature—hot. High temperatures are the rule, although Scorpio (the other sign ruled by Mars) can also give extreme weather which may be cold. Wind—fairly windy, will add to a windy planet's influence. Moisture—dry. If other aspects in force show rain, aspects from Aries will contribute violence, stormy conditions. The Moon adversely aspecting from Aries brings violence.

TAURUS. Temperature—moderating, similar in effect to its ruler, Venus; it will warm things up in cold weather or cool the atmosphere in hot, brings temperatures best for growing crops. Wind—calm. It is a fixed sign and one in which planets tend to produce weather in which not a breath of air stirs. Aspects to the wind ascendant from this sign will tend to prevent winds. Moisture— wet. The Moon is exalted in Taurus. Aspects of wet planets from this sign will give growing rains of a generous quantity, steady rains for a day or two.

GEMINI. Temperature—cold, favoring rapid changes, a cold and drafty influence not as cold as Capricorn and Aquarius but colder than Pisces. Wind—extremely windy, the windiest of all the signs; Virgo comes a close second. Virtually any planet aspecting from this sign will initiate lively winds. Storm combinations with this influence will have considerable wind accompaniment. Moisture— quite dry, doesn't favor rain and even tends to eliminate cloudiness or fog by blowing them away. This influence in a rainstorm will indicate a driving rain or a rain that is secondary to a windstorm.

CANCER. Temperature—moderately cold; not so cold as Capricorn and Aquarius but colder than Pisces. It contributes low temperatures. Wind—calm. The ruler is the Moon, but the influence

is toward quietness in aspects formed from this sign. Moisture —
wet. This is the wettest sign. Scorpio may at times give more violence
in its downpours, but Cancer brings a tendency to steady and
voluminous rains. In strong aspects, the rain can come down for
days at a time, full force.

LEO. Temperature—hot. When this sign influence is in force,
it brings hot weather in which not a breath of air stirs, sweltering
weather. Even in winter, where this influences the temperature
strongly, it can bring bright, sunshiny days that melt snow and
drive the snow clouds from the skies. Wind—still, almost as quiet
as Taurus. It tends to stifle wind. In the spring, it may cause trees
and plants to bud and sprout prematurely, only to be killed by later
cold or freezes. Moisture—dry, will delay rain and parch the earth.
If the other indications are strong enough to bring rain in spite of
Leo's influence, it will contribute lightning and violence.

VIRGO. Temperature—cold. It tends to contribute dry and
cold influence. Blustery weather is typical. Wind—quite windy,
variable as to force and direction. Cutting winds that chill to the
bone are characteristic. Moisture—dry, uniformly so. It discourages
excessive wind or fog; but when other influences contribute strong
wind indications, it can add violence. Grains and cereal crops mature
well under beneficial aspects from this sign.

LIBRA. Temperature—cool. The influence here is toward the
lower temperatures but not extremes. Wind—quite windy, will
contribute to wind violence in stormy conditions; it can also
contribute to the formation of a tornado or hurricane. If the aspects
are favorable, it will bring cool, refreshing winds. Moisture—dry or
drying. If nothing contradicts, it will favor dry weather, tends to
blow clouds from the sky and give bright, sunshiny days favorable
for outside work (or kite flying).

SCORPIO. Temperature—extremist, either towards heat or cold,
depending on other influences at work. Never expect moderation
from aspects from this sign. Wind—violence. If the aspect indicates
wind or even breezes, this sign will increase winds to violence and
breezes to strong winds; it is a strong contributor to storm
indications. Moisture—wet, not an indication to rely on to break a
drought. If further dry weather is indicated, this only extends it. If
wet weather is indicated, this sign with other strong indicators of
wet weather will bring cloudbursts and downpours. Typical weather
otherwise is to bring heat and still, sultry days and nights which

make sleep difficult and work almost impossible.

SAGITTARIUS. Temperature—warm, mild. The influence is to bright, clear, sunshiny days. It tends to make for exceptional visibility. Haze, even smog will succumb to a good aspect from this sign. Wind—moderately windy, neither encourages nor discourages storm winds. Moisture—dry, inhibits rain and cloudiness. Typical weather is fine, favoring outdoor sports and picnicking.

CAPRICORN. Temperature—extremely cold, the sign of storms and extreme cold weather. It is a contributor to destructive floods and droughts. In the winter, the inclination is to temperatures low enough to be destructive to life. In summer heat, don't expect this to moderate; on the contrary, it will just become more miserable. Wind—windy, increases the force of winds indicated; it brings blizzards in winter, destructive snowstorms. In summer, it can contribute to hailstorms. Moisture—wet. It brings disagreeable conditions; dark, damp, cold days; and cold, drenching rains. Don't look for this influence to break a drought; it will tend to increase drought. Unseasonable weather of all types can be attributed to this influence. Any time of year, if storm is indicated, this sign will increase the destructiveness. Typical weather produced by this influence: temperature drops below zero, wind rises to gale force, driving sleet and snow before it.

AQUARIUS. Temperature—extreme cold. It consistently indicates a drop of temperature. Dry, crisp, cold weather is characteristic. In summer, it will indicate a cool spell. Only when other aspects are violent will Aquarius contribute to a storm. Wind —breezy. Moderate breezes are typical; but if violent aspects are from this sign, it will make for driving winds and excessive cold, with snow in blinding flurries. Moisture—dry. Typically favors dry weather; but if other aspects indicate moisture or rain, this adds lightning and electrical displays.

PISCES. Temperature—cold, a consistent influence for lower temperatures. The influence is gentle and mild. Wind—calm, tends to moderate whatever windy elements are present. Moisture—wet. In a combination that indicates storms, this merely shows that considerable rain will accompany what violence is shown. When free from extreme influences, this sign causes rains which are seasonable and are of benefit to growing things.

PEARCE'S WEATHER BITS

Highlights - *Condensed from*
The Textbook of Astrology
book 3, AstroMeteorology
by Alfred John Pearce

By their science the Egyptian astrologers could foretell years of scarcity and plenty, pestilence, earthquakes, inundations, and the appearance of comets, and do many other things surpassing the sagacity of the vulgar.

The State-endowed Meteorologic Office frequently fails to foretell the general character of the weather only twenty-four hours in advance, and dare not attempt to forecast the general character of a coming season.

Archimedes discovered the law of specific gravity; and Galileo discovered the law, which is the basis of mechanics. The laws of Kepler, as they are called from their discoverer, are 3 important general facts in astrology.

1. The orbits of the planets are ellipses, with the Sun in one of the foci.
2. The planets move over equal areas in equal times.
3. The squares of the times of revolution of any 2 planets are to each other in the same proportion as the cubes of their mean distances from the Sun. (This 3rd law may justly be regarded as the most remarkable and the most pregnant with important consequences.

Kepler found from pure observation that the ancients were right when they averred that "sublunary natures are excited by the conjunctions and aspects of the planets."

An aspect is an angle formed on the earth by the luminous beams of two planets, of strength to stir up the virtue of sublunary things. When two of the heavenly bodies are in conjunction or opposition, they have nearly the same declination, and act powerfully on the earth and its atmosphere, because they attract in the same line; they rise, culminate, and set nearly together, when in conjunction; when in opposition, one rises as the other sets, one is in the upper when the other is in the lower meridian.

Observation shows that certain of the celestial bodies are in certain relative positions when excess of heat or drought prevails, excess of cold or moisture prevails. .... hence,

1. That the said positions of those celestial bodies are the original, though not the proximate, causes of such atmospheric phenomena.
2. That, since the periods at which such celestial positions shall recur can always be accurately computed, it is possible to foretell the periods concurrent therewith, at which such atmospheric phenomena will also recur.

It is observed that when Mercury is in conjunction with the Sun, the atmosphere is greatly disturbed, and the wind is strong; in winter, hurricanes sometimes happen, as in Dec. 1863.

Search for the causes of variations in the seasons — of a hot or a cool summer, of a severe or a mild winter — and of the visitations of drought, floods, storms, etc.

When Sun is in conjunction, parallel, opposition, sextile, quartile or trine aspect with Jupiter, the weather is warm and is usually fine except in aspect to Saturn or Uranus.

The author said Sun Spots will never lead to the discovery of the laws regulating the weather.

Moon

Great changes of weather are often found to occur when the Moon is in major aspect with the Sun and one or more of the larger planets simultaneously. Hence the following aphorisms were compiled two centuries since:

"If the Moon after conjunction or opposition with the Sun, immediately apply to Saturn, especially in water signs, rain shall follow."

"If the Moon apply to Jupiter, fine weather, with hardly any rain will follow."

"If the Moon apply to Mars, rain will follow, unless Mars be in Aries, Leo, or Sagittarius, or in aspect with Jupiter. If Mars be in aspect with Venus or Saturn, much rain will follow."

"If the new Moon apply to Venus, without doubt rain will follow, unless she is in aspect with Jupiter. If Venus be in aspect with Saturn or Uranus, cold, rain, or snow according to the season will follow."

"If the new Moon apply to Mercury retrograde, rain will follow. If Mercury be with Venus or Saturn, much rain. If with Mars or Jupiter, warm or dry weather may be expected. Brisk winds will follow."

Out of 760 rains, 646 began when the Moon was very near the upper or lower meridian, or very near rising or setting. (Angles)

Changes of weather take place more frequently at the first quarter and the last sextile than at any other period of lunations-but the nature of the change depends on the planet with which the Sun and Moon may be configurated at.

Jupiter

Jupiter is fruitful and airy, and expressly connected with winds proceeding from the north. The position of Jupiter in the western angle at the vernal equinox of 1864 was followed by a remarkably fine, warm and dry season.

If Jupiter be in an angle at a solstice or an equinox, or receive the application of the Moon at new moon, a temperate, good and wholesome air and a season favourable to the increase and fructifying of that which is sown and planted in the earth will follow. The ancients held that the action of Jupiter was varied in signs. When in Cancer, Aquarius or Pisces, more rain falls.

Saturn

When Saturn is in aspect to the Sun, the action is to condense aqueous vapor, to lower the temperature of the air. In contrast to Jupiter's health giving breezes, Saturn brings bleak, bronchitis-producing easterly winds or a stagnant, mephitic atmosphere favoring the spread of fevers. Spring blossoms can be blighted or, if summer, crops are injured.

When Saturn crosses the equator; the atmosphere is greatly disturbed. (once every 15 yrs).

Mars

Mars when in an angle at the equinox or solstice promotes evaporation and raises the temperature, causing a drier state of the weather than Jupiter, particularly when in Aries, Leo, or Cancer.

When Mars is in conjunction or opposition with Sun, calorific influence is usually observed to extend over a period of 2 to 5 days before the completion of the aspect, and a reaction frequently takes place immediately after.

Mars when in power generally causes such mischief and destruction as are concomitant with dryness. The atmosphere parched by hot, pestilential, and blasting winds, accompanied by drought. At sea, ships suddenly wrecked by the turbulence of the wind and strokes of lightning. Rivers fail and springs dry up.

Mars in Leo has power. Close to the meridian in Leo, stationary, the winter quarter was fair and mild, and the driest of the century in England for solstice Dec. 22, 1883.

Venus

Venus exerts a temperate and moist influence when in one of the angles at the equinox or solstice, when in conjunction and parallel declination with the Sun, and when in the equator.

Mercury

The electric planet (some say) produces rapid changes of weather. It generates in the atmosphere turbulent, sharp and variable winds. This if in conjunction or opposition with Mars, Jupiter or Saturn and especially if at the same time in or near the equator of tropics or in sign Scorpio or Leo or with Sun and Moon at eclipse.

The Sun in conjunction with Mercury is more prone to send us a hurricane than the Sun with Venus.

Mercury was in the 4th angle and nearly sextile aspect with Uranus. The fearfully severe winter followed with terrible blizzards with appalling loss of life. (Dec. 21, 1887 in Washington.)

Uranus

Disturbance caused by Uranus usually sets in very suddenly and can take shape of hailstorms. Tends to condense aqueous vapors and to lower the temperature of the air. Uranus in the 4th angle seems to threaten much damage by storms, more particularly in Scotland.

Neptune

There is evidence that Neptune in the equator disturbed the weather. Neptune in the 4th angle brought a cold and wet summer disastrous for farmers.

Mutual conjunctions and oppositions of the Planets

Mars and Saturn when in conjunction, more particularly when their declinations are the same and when the Moon happens to be in the same position cause a turbulent state of atmosphere. Conjunction of Mars and Saturn brought great winds and sometimes rain at any season of the year (in Cancer, Scorpio or Pisces). Thunder lightning, also inundations.

Dr. Goad records a dreadful tempest, wind, rain, and hail on the 13th of Nov. 1664 in England following the conjunction of Mars and Saturn in Sagittarius 27 degrees on the 12th. This combination produces storms and great disturbance of weather.

Jupiter and Saturn disturb the weather very greatly. Once every 20 years. Produces cold and dry weather, occasionally fogs. Mars and Jupiter do not always raise the temperature and promote evaporation. In Aries — great cold; in Taurus, snow; and in Leo, great cold.

Venus with Saturn produces either cold weather or much downfall; frequently fog, and sometimes strong gales.

Mercury with Mars is productive of vehement winds. Mercury with Jupiter frequently produces strong winds, and usually raises the temperature, sometimes thunderstorms.

Venus with Mars on the whole inclining more to warmth then cold. Overlook none of the conjunctions. When 3 or more planets are near together in longitude, great disturbance of the atmosphere is found to result.

A BRIEF HISTORY OF ASTROMETEOROLOGY

By George J. McCormack

The first known work on weather and the atmosphere was The Meteorologica by the Greek philosopher-scientist Aristotle (384 BC to 322 BC). His pupil, Theophratus expanded this early treatise in two works "On Winds" and "On the Signs of Rain, Winds, Storms and Fair Weather."

These were the sole authorities on meteorology until scientific investigations began in the 17th century. (Ptolemy's Tetrabiblos, 152 AD quoted brief excerpts).

In 1686, Dr. J. Goad's Astro-Meteorologica, based on 39 years of his own astro-weather observations and correlations was published in London. Until the end of the 19th Century this text was the leading authority on the subject. It includes a transcript of astronomer Johannes Kepler's diary of astro-weather observations from June 28, 1617 to August 9, 1629. Here Kepler expounded some of his theories relating planetary phenomena to atmospheric changes. It is a matter of historical record that he attained recognition for his remarkably accurate long-range weather forecasting long before advancing his laws of planetary motion. Kepler's "Mysterium Cosmographicam" is a fully documented record of his work from 1602 to 1629. Some scientists who have written disparagingly of the renowned Kepler's interest in correlating planetary phenomena to terrestrial events have rendered a disservice to the progress of science.

Critically tested astro-weather forecasts during the last century, ventured for various parts of the world more than a year in advance, support and confirm Kepler's theories. He discovered that additional magnetic angles of 30,45, 135, and 150 degrees between celestial bodies synchronized perfectly with atmospheric reactions.

Commander R.J. Morrison of the Royal Navy, publisher of the world known <u>Zadkiel's Almanac</u> more than a century ago, further refined his predecessors' discoveries with a more modern scientific approach.

Morrison's successor, Dr. Alfred J. Pearce (1840-1923), continued the <u>Almanac</u> from 1876 for forty years. He also published his "Weather Guide" in London during 1864, the <u>Science of the Stars</u> in 1881, and completed a magnum opus - his <u>Textbook</u> Vol. II in 1889. In this expanded work, Pearce evolved new techniques from his own observations with detailed instructions in the method. He cited case histories and voluminous data to support and rationalize the theory of astrometeorology.

Observations of solar radiation and sunspots will never lead to the discovery of the laws which regulate the weather. The atmosphere is often liable to unusual and long continued impressions, and these are induced by planetary action on the earth as well as on the Sun. Based on many years of specialized experiences with astrometeorology, we are convinced that to abandon this research is to render the discovery of the laws that regulate the weather, hopeless.

From Astrotech Weather Guide *by George J. McCormack, 1965*

CHAPTER XXIII
THE EFFECTS OF SOLAR ECLIPSES

From **Mundane Astrology**, *by Raphael.*

The following are the principal effects of Solar eclipses when falling in the decanates of each sign.

Aries.

First decanate.—War, tumults, seditions and controversies, motion of armies, and an inclination of the air to excessive drought.

Second decanate.—Imprisonment and sadness of some king, and danger of death to him; the corruption of trees bearing fruit, and of things growing on the earth.

Third decanate.—Grief and sadness to mortals, death of !some great woman, and destruction of cattle.

Taurus.

First decanate—Afflicts, trade and business, and destroys corn and food crops.

Second decanate.—Causes danger to travellers, and to women in childbirth.

Third decanate.—Brings pestilence and famine.

Gemini.

First decanate.—Dissension and strife among clergy and religious denominations; also causes hatred, neglect and contempt for the laws of God and man.

Second decanate.—Causes piracies, thefts and murders.

Third decanate.—Death of some king, and many troubles to the country.

Cancer.

First decanate.—Disturbs the air, and causes great changes and alterations in the weather.

Second decanate.—Dries up rivers and fountains, and stirs up incontinency and wantonness among women.

Third decanate.—Sedition, pestilence and much disease.

Leo.

First decanate.—Denotes the death of some famous prince, and scarcity of corn.

Second decanate.—Many troubles, anxieties to kings, princes and great men.

Third decanate.—Profanation of holy places, churches, and sacred edifices: captivity, besieging and ransacking of towns.

Virgo.

First decanate.—It denotes great calamity, and death of some king.

Second decanate.—Famine, pestilence and sedition.

Third decanate.—Great troubles and adversity, probably imprisonment to painters, poets, and to those who live by their wits.

Libra.

First decanate.—Corrupts the air, causes pestilence, and a scarcity and dearness of corn.

Second decanate.—It portends the death of a great king, sedition and famine,

Third decanate.—Trouble to the nobility and detriment to their estates.

Scorpio.

First decanate.—Causes war, tumults, slaughter, captivity and treason.

Second decanate.—Mischief to some peace-loving king.

Third decanate.—The rise of a tyrant, and idleness and slothfulness of the former king, hateful to all.

Sagittarius.

First decanate.—Much dissension and hatred among men.

Second decanate.—Deaths of camels, and such cattle as chew the cud.

Third decanate.—Variously affects horses and armies.

Capricorn.

First decanate.—Unhappiness to great men, the transmigration of some king, and the rebellion of nobles and common people.

Second decanate.—Causes military riots, and the mutiny of soldiers against their officers.

Third decanate.—It induces the tumultuary motion of some king, and causes famines.

Aquarius.

First decanate.—It causes public grief and sorrow.

Second decanate.—Public robberies, thefts, rapes, earthquakes and famine.

Third decanate.—The death and slaughter of sheep and beasts of the field.

Pisces.

First decanate.—Dries up rivers and makes the sea-coast unfortunate.

Second decanate.—Causes the death of some famous and excellent man; the destruction of fish, tidal waves and inundations.

Third decanate.—Sedition, cruelty, fierceness and inhumanity of soldiers.

CHAPTER XXIV.

THE EFFECTS OF LUNAR ECLIPSES

The following are the principal effects of Lunar eclipses when falling in the decanates of each sign.

Aries.

First decanate.—Fevers, incendiarism, firing of woods and forests, and dryness of the air.

Second decanate.—Pestilence.

Third decanate.—Causes abortive births, incommodities, and dangers to women.

Taurus.

First decanate.—Death and diseases among cattle.

Second decanate.—Death of some queen, and a scarcity of seeds, and barrenness of the earth.

Third decanate.—Chief effects will be manifest among snakes and creeping things, which will perish by the million.

Gemini

First decanate.—Threatens incursions and rapines of enemies.

Second decanate.—Brings sudden motion of armies, and the solicitation of private and public bodies.

Third decanate.—Causes death of some illustrious and renowned man.

Cancer.

First decanate.—Excites and stirs up wars.

Second decanate.—Causes grievous exactions, intolerable tributes, taxes and such like burdens.

Third decanate.—Brings death to the female sex; sudden destruction and miseries.

Leo.

First decanate.—Brings the sudden infirmity of some king; or the death of a great man.

Second decanate.—Journey of the king, and mutation of things.

Third decanate.—Stirs up the people and armies to new attempts at sedition and insurrection.

Virgo.

First decanate.—Causes sickness and infirmities to the king, and various seditions and discords among men.

Second decanate.—Brings damage to councillors and scribes, and the like.

Third decanate.—Causes diseases among human beings.

Libra.

First decanate.—Provokes furious storms of hail.

Second decanate.—Pernicious to everyone.

Third decanate.—Threatens the death of some renowned and illustrious man.

Scorpio.

First decanate.—It portends horrible thunders and lightnings and perhaps an earthquake.

Second decanate.—It dries up olives and fruits, and the air is contagent with fevers and pestilence.

Third decanate.—Brings the same, also sharp sicknesses, with many seditions, quarrels and slaughters.

Sagittarius.

First decanate.—Brings thefts and rapines.

Second decanate.—Brings destruction to horses and mules.

Third decanate.—Causes pestilence and many evils among mankind.

Capricorn.

First decanate.—Causes conspiracies among men, and shows the lamentable murder of some excellent man.

Second decanate.—Brings frequent incursions and assaults of soldiers, robberies and captivities.

Third decanate.—Causes the death of some king, and also sedition.

Aquarius.

First decanate.—Shows sickness of some king.

Second decanate.—It universally damages the seeds of the earth.

Third decanate.—Causes a change in all things.

Pisces.

First decanate.—Brings sorrow to the priests and to religious houses.

Second decanate.—Brings death to some great and illustrious person.

Third decanate.—Threatens robberies and promiscuous assaults and rapines, both on sea and land.

Editor's note: The delineations given by Sepharial are much the same. I used Raphael because it was to hand. Taking a cue from McCormack, we would expect eclipses to produce results in those longitudes where they fall on the MC/IC axis, the timing of such events to be triggered by aspecting or ruling planets making exact aspects. Page 99, Zadkiel's interpretation of a solar eclipse in the first decanate of Taurus as affecting potatoes is a free interpretation, based on Taurus's rulership of starchy root crops, and the prevalence of such crops in the areas affected.

Bibliography
(*new to the 2012 edition*)

Broughton, Luke, *The Elements of Astrology* (New York: the author, 1898)

Egan, Carolyn, *Weathersage* (Rhode Island: Weathersage.com)

Green, H.S., Raphael, Carter, C.E.O., *Mundane Astrology, The Astrology of Nations and States, three volumes in one* (Bel Air, MD: Astrology Classics, 2004).

Hazelrigg, John, *Astrosophic Principles* (New York: Hermetic Pub. Co., 1917)

Pearce, A.J., *The Text-Book of Astrology* (Tempe, AZ: American Federation of Astrologers, 2006)

Ptolemy, Claudius, *Tetrabiblos,* translated by J.M. Ashmand (Bel Air, MD: Astrology Classics, 2002)

Raman, B.V., *Astrology in Predicting Weather and Earthquakes* (New Delhi: UBSPD, 2011).

Riske, Kris Brandt, *Astrometeorology, Planetary Powers in Weather Forecasting* (Tempe, AZ: American Federation of Astrologers, 1997).

Sepharial (Gorn-Old, Walter), *Eclipses* (London: L.N. Fowler, 1915).

Weber, Lind, *The Astro-Geology of Earthquakes and Volcanoes* (Tempe, AZ: American Federation of Astrologers, 1994).

Zain, C.C., *Course 15: Weather Predicting, The Hermetic System of Astrological Weather Analysis* (Albuquerque, N.M.: Church of Light, 2011).

About the Author:

George J. McCormack was born on April 26, 1887 at 9:16 pm LMT at Springfield, MA. In addition to pursuing a full time career in the Engineering Department of the New York Bell Telephone Company, "Gee-Jay" McCormack became one of the leading figures in American astrology. He first became interested in the subject in 1906, and ultimately specialized in Astrometeorology, Financial Astrology, and Mundane Astrology. With an evident gift for organization, he was a co-founder of the American Academy of Astrologicans in 1916, organized the Astrologer's Guild in 1926, and was co-founder of the AFA in 1938. He served as Vice President of the AFA in 1940 and 1941 and was its President in 1942. Later in the decade, he served as President of the American Academy of Astrologicians.

McCormack published and edited "Astrotech Weekly" from 1933 to 1941 and was a professional astrologer at Jersey City Heights 1935-39 and at Fairlawn, New Jersey, thereafter. His weather forecasts were publicized in Telephone Company house organs, as well as in astrological publications. During the latter half of his life, he was considered to be the leading authority on Astrometeorology.

Mrs. McCormack predeceased him in 1969. They had one son, who did not pursue astrology.

— From <u>Astrological Pioneers of America</u>, by James H. Holden and Robert A. Hughes, AFA, 1988. Used by permission. A note with this entry says the original edition of this book was limited to 100 copies.

Better books make better astrologers.
Here are some of our other titles:

AstroAmerica's Daily Ephemeris, 2010-2020
AstroAmerica's Daily Ephemeris, 2000-2020
 - *both for Midnight. Compiled & formatted by David R. Roell*

Al Biruni
The Book of Instructions in the Elements of the Art of Astrology, *1029 AD,*
 translated by R. Ramsay Wright

David Anrias
Man and the Zodiac

Derek Appleby
Horary Astrology: The Art of Astrological Divination

E.H. Bailey
The Prenatal Epoch

Joseph Blagrave
Astrological Practice of Physick

C.E.O. Carter
The Astrology of Accidents
An Encyclopaedia of Psychological Astrology
Essays on the Foundations of Astrology
The Principles of Astrology, *Intermediate no. 1*
Some Principles of Horoscopic Delineation, *Intermediate no. 2*
Symbolic Directions in Modern Astrology
The Zodiac and the Soul

Charubel & Sepharial
Degrees of the Zodiac Symbolized, *1898*

H.L. Cornell
Encyclopaedia of Medical Astrology

Nicholas Culpeper
Astrological Judgement of Diseases from the Decumbiture of the Sick, *1655,*
 and, **Urinalia**, *1658*

Dorotheus of Sidon
Carmen Astrologicum, *c. 50 AD, translated by David Pingree*

Nicholas deVore
Encyclopedia of Astrology

Firmicus Maternus
Ancient Astrology Theory & Practice: Matheseos Libri VIII,
c. 350 AD, translated by Jean Rhys Bram

Margaret Hone
The Modern Text-Book of Astrology

Alan Leo
The Progressed Horoscope, *1905*
The Key to Your Own Nativity, *1910*
Dictionary of Astrology, *edited by Vivian Robson, 1929*

William Lilly
Christian Astrology, books 1 & 2, *1647*
  The Introduction to Astrology, Resolution of all manner of questions.
Christian Astrology, book 3, *1647*
  Easie and plaine method teaching how to judge upon nativities.

Jean-Baptiste Morin
The Cabal of the Twelve Houses Astrological
  translated by George Wharton, edited by D.R. Roell

Claudius Ptolemy
Tetrabiblos, *c. 140 AD, translated by J.M. Ashmand*

Vivian Robson
Astrology and Sex
Electional Astrology
Fixed Stars & Constellations in Astrology
A Beginner's Guide to Practical Astrology
A Student's Text-Book of Astrology,
  Vivian Robson Memorial Edition

Diana Roche
The Sabian Symbols, A Screen of Prophecy

David Roell
Skeet Shooting for Astrologers

Richard Saunders
The Astrological Judgement and Practice of Physick, *1677*

Sepharial
The Manual of Astrology, the Standard Work
Primary Directions, a definitive study
Sepharial On Money. *For the first time in one volume, complete texts:*
  • **Law of Values**
  • **Silver Key**
  • **Arcana, or Stock and Share Key** — *first time in print!*

Zane Stein
Essence and Application, A View from Chiron

James Wilson, Esq.
Dictionary of Astrology

H.S. Green, Raphael & C.E.O. Carter
Mundane Astrology: *3 Books, complete in one volume.*

If not available from your local bookseller, order directly from:
The Astrology Center of America
207 Victory Lane
Bel Air, MD 21014

on the web at:
http://www.astroamerica.com

www.ingramcontent.com/pod-product-compliance
Lightning Source LLC
Chambersburg PA
CBHW021334090426
42742CB00008B/597